with history
with history
with history
with history
with history
with history
with history
with history
with history

Corres

with history
with history
with history
with history
with history
with history
with history
with history
with history
with history
with history

ponding

The Art & Benefits of Collecting Autographs

John E. Schlimm II

Library of Congress Cataloging-in-Publication Data

Schlimm, John E., 1971-
    Corresponding with history : the art & benefits of collecting autographs / John E. Schlimm II.
        p.   cm.
    ISBN 0-88280-130-9 (cloth ed.). -- ISBN 0-88280-131-7 (softcover ed.)
    1. Autographs--Collectors and collecting--United States.
I. Title
Z41.S35   1997
 929.8'8'075--dc20   96-21682
                                                        CIP
                                                         AC

****

Cover design by John E. Schlimm and John E. Schlimm II

****

Published by ETC Publications
      Palm Springs
      California 92262

Published in the United States of America.

The ASAP Children's Assistance Fund

A percentage of the royalties from this book will be donated to the ASAP Children's Assistance Fund headquartered just outside of Washington, D.C.

The Children's Assistance Fund in part raises money to buy holiday gifts for children who are both **infected and affected** by the AIDS epidemic. One or both parents of these children are HIV-positive, which means the children will most likely be orphaned before they reach adulthood! The program also provides emergency financial assistance, counseling, and a care-givers network.

The program was founded in 1989 by Shepherd and Anita Smith, who started by serving two children in two states. By 1995, the Children's Assistance Fund was distributing gifts to more than 10,000 children around the United States who might not have otherwise received a gift. This number is expected to grow more and more every year.

By purchasing a copy of <u>Corresponding With History</u>, you are helping to bring a smile to the face of a child during the holiday season and, indeed, year round.

Let's unite and show these beautiful little boys and girls that they have a friend to walk this road with them!

If you would like to know more about the ASAP Children's Assistance Fund, you can write or call:

> The ASAP Children's Assistance Fund
> P.O. Box 17433
> Washington, D.C. 20041
>
> (703) 471-7350

> Thank you so much for your help!
>
> John E. Schlimm II

I WOULD LIKE TO DEDICATE THIS BOOK TO THE FOLLOWING PEOPLE WHO HAVE INFLUENCED MY LIFE...

Mom and Dad
Who always taught me to chase my dreams
And
To do it my way

Grandma Schlimm
I started writing this book the day after her funeral
I'll love you always
X O X O X O X O X O X O X O X O X O X O X

Sally Aman
Communications Director/Press Secretary to Mrs. Tipper Gore
Who for eight months shared history with me
And
Showed me what it means to be the best!
You'll always have my greatest respect and admiration

Mrs. Tipper Gore and Mrs. Susan Allen
Two of my favorite Ladies!
I only wish there could be a Gore/Allen Ticket

Stevie, Jon, Paul, Daryl, Emily, and Kathleen
Best Friends Forever!

Roland
Whatever!

PROLOGUE

I was born and raised in a small town nestled in the Allegheny Mountains of Northwestern Pennsylvania. My heart and home will always be in St. Marys, Pennsylvania, but I discovered a whole other world waiting just beyond the mountain range. In August 1990, I started four years at Marymount University in Arlington, Virginia, next to our nation's capital. And thus, the adventure began...

If what you are about to read seems unbelievable for a college kid, be assured that even now as I sit back home in St. Marys, after more than 1,460 days and over 1,000 autographs later, it still is a little bit hard for me to believe. Luckily, I have the photographs and the autographs to prove I did those things and I was there...

John E. Schlimm II
St. Marys, Pennsylvania

September 1994

CONTENTS

All autographs, photographs, letters, and drawings displayed in this book are from the collection of John E. Schlimm II

INTRODUCTION

This book is about my experiences in autograph collecting. I have learned a great deal on my own and I want to share those lessons with you, whether you are thinking about starting a collection or already have one. Over the past few years, I have amassed over one thousand autographs ranging in every genre. Autograph collecting is a most exciting and educational hobby for no other pursuit offers as much direct access to the people and places of which history is made.

I have had many exciting adventures while collecting autographs; adventures spanning two Presidential Administrations, which have introduced me to a world beyond my wildest dreams. My most exciting and rewarding endeavor was an eight month internship I served in Mrs. Tipper Gore's Office at The White House where I worked directly with Mrs. Gore's Communications Director/Press Secretary, Sally Aman, for whom I have the greatest respect and admiration. While at The White House, I had the unique opportunity to watch history in the making and briefly partake in that history. I came away from the experience with a small piece of history, manifested through autographs.

I am happy to share my stories to show how exciting autograph collecting can be. With each experience and each new autograph, I learned a new lesson about collecting signatures and I learned more about the world in which we live.

Autograph collecting is an educational hobby. There is no better or more thrilling way to learn about historical figures or other celebrities than to meet or write those very people and ask for signed photos, books, and other information. For this reason and because I believe in making academic learning as fun and as beneficial as possible, I have dedicated a section of this book to school projects. I want to help teachers, both in school and in the home, incorporate autograph collecting into their course curriculums. I hope teachers will find my entire book helpful if they choose to make their classes more stimulating by encouraging their students to correspond directly with the figures they most admire and, in the process, become a part of history themselves.

To me, each autograph is an original work of art created by the signer. Each signature is unique and each represents a tiny piece of history; a history of which you can be a part by collecting autographs.

𝒫art 1

THE WHITE HOUSE

July 13, 1992

Dear John Schlimm,

What a very good Marquette commencement speech you wrote with me in mind, and how impressed I am by your talent and enterprise! The central ideas you expressed so well were also important in my remarks, and I am gratified to know that a gifted young person like you shares the values that mean so much to me.

Thank you so much for thinking of me in such an eloquent way, and please keep writing. George Bush and I love to be reminded -- as you have reminded me -- that America's future is in very good hands.

With all best wishes for a rich and rewarding life,

Warmly,

Barbara Bush

The first political autograph I ever received

POLITICAL AUTOGRAPHS

Political autographs are my favorite genre to collect. Since politics is a high profile profession, we, as a nation, can publicly watch politicians make their climb toward the top and, on occasion, their fall back to the bottom. Political autographs represent the essence and history of these successes and failures.

Although I enjoy collecting signatures from various genres, I found it wisest to choose the category I liked the most and concentrate on it. Therefore, I set out to get as many political signatures as possible.

The first political autograph I ever received was a signed letter from First Lady Barbara Bush in 1992. Since then, I have written to politicians from each of the three branches of the U.S. Government and beyond. These politicians include all of the Presidents and First Ladies, Vice Presidents and Second Ladies, all one hundred U.S. Senators, various members of the U.S. House of Representatives, all fifty Governors and spouses, the nine Supreme Court Justices and a few retired Justices, current and former Cabinet members, candidates, and various other public officials. I have also grouped military leaders and astronauts into this category as most of these men and women are closely associated with the world of politics.

I have been fortunate through several experiences in Washington to obtain some of these autographs in person. One lesson you quickly learn in Washington is that politicians are constantly being recycled from one election year to the next: A former Governor may end up as Secretary of the Interior or a former White House Chief of Staff may move on to be a talk show host. If you cannot get a political figure's authentic autograph at one job, you may be able to easily obtain it at their next workplace.

I cannot stress enough the educational benefit of writing to these historical figures. Not only do politicians embody history, both past and present, but through writing to these people I have learned about that history. This has aided me in my own college career and continues to be a great personal tutor on the "who, what, where, when, why, and how" of modern history.

The educational reward can be increased by also requesting a biography of the person to whom you are writing. Not only is this informative, but it makes a nice addition to your collection. Almost every politician and celebrity has copies of their biography ready to send to fans.

One term that you should become familiar with is the Franking Privilege, which allows Members of Congress, Presidents, and other high ranking officials in the national government to mail items free of charge. This is signified with a facsimile of the official's signature(frank) in place of a stamp. This unique method of postage makes the envelopes collectable and worth saving.

An autograph collector's worst enemy is the Autopen. This machine is a lifesaver for political offices, but a nuisance for serious autograph collectors. The Autopen mechanically copies a person's signature on letters and just about anything else. Some Autopen signatures are hard to identify unless you have two of the person's autographs to compare. I have found in my experience with Autopen signatures that they are sometimes shaky looking. However, the Autopen is a convenience in offices that has helped to cut down on the items an official has to personally sign.

The human equivalent to the Autopen in many offices is an assistant or some other staff member who is authorized to sign their boss' name. These signatures are often difficult to tell from an authentic autograph unless you are an expert. I have adopted the policy that if I receive an autograph, as long as it is not an Autopen signature, facsimile, or stamp, I am not going to ask any questions and I will just assume it is the real thing.

Since politicians get large volumes of mail sent to them, it is in your best interest to find out the name of someone in their office who might be a more direct contact for getting your request to the actual politician. For example, it is better to send your request via an Executive Assistant, who has daily contact with an official, than sending it directly to the politician since it will then most likely end up in a pile of other similar letters.

The best advice I can give you concerning every genre of autographs is if you ever have the chance to meet a celebrity, regardless of who they are or how famous they are, get their autograph. This is especially so in politics for you never know which politician might turn out to be the next star. If you should get the rare chance of meeting with the President or Vice President ask for an autograph. A face-to-face meeting is usually the only way you will get an authentic signature!

It can also be fun to send politicians cards on their birthdays or at Christmas as most of them send out Christmas cards with pictures of their families to friends and supporters. This would be an interesting addition to your collection or would make a great collection of its own. Members of the U.S. Congress also have a limited edition set of trading cards which they occasionally send to autograph seekers. This would make a most interesting collection, especially if the cards are signed. I received one such autographed card from Senator James Jeffords of Vermont. Since there is only a limited number available, these cards are difficult to get, but worth a try.

By far, my favorite autographs in this genre are those of the First Ladies, which I will write about a little later. However, the top goal in collecting political signatures is to acquire an autograph from a current or former President of the United States. These men's signatures are among the most difficult to obtain.

CHAPTER 1
THE EXECUTIVE BRANCH

<u>The President of the United States</u>

As the headquarters for the Executive Branch of the U.S. Government, The White House receives millions of letters requesting autographs and other items from the First Family. It is impossible for the President to comply with all of these demands, especially the numerous requests for his autograph.

The Correspondence Office at The White House is extremely well organized with staffers, volunteers, and interns who open, sort, and organize the mail into various categories ranging from autograph requests to constituent complaints. These letters are sent to the appropriate offices where they can be efficiently answered. The majority of letters never make it to the President's desk. What this means for an autograph seeker is that instead of receiving an authentically signed photo, you will most likely be sent the President's official portrait with a facsimile of his signature at the bottom.

Although a copy of the President's signature is not exactly what you want, it is still exciting to receive a package from The White House. These photographs by themselves are very collectable, especially if the portrait changes or when a different Administration comes into office. I have seen White House portraits of former and current Presidents for sale in many souvenir shops. These are the same pictures The White House mails to collectors during a particular Administration.

The White House has a variety of photographs of the President that are sent to constituents. When I interned at The White House, I not only got the President's official portrait, but I was also given a photo of him speaking and a picture of him and Mrs. Clinton on the steps of Air Force I. You can also write and receive a picture of Air Force I and Air Force II, which are the official planes that carry the President and Vice President, respectively. Portraits of the White House are also available.

The best way to get a President's autograph is to find out who might be a future President. Looking back on history, we can find examples of politicians at almost every level of government who eventually became President. Almost immediately following a Presidential election, speculation begins as to who will run in four years. These are the names you want to listen for and the people to whom you want to write letters.

I have had the distinct honor of meeting President Bush and President

Clinton. The first time I met President Clinton I was at a 1993 staff birthday party for his wife, First Lady Hillary Rodham Clinton. I did not ask for an autograph since interns and staffers are discouraged from doing so and I can understand the reason. It would be like someone asking you for your autograph in your own home. It was a thrill just to meet and speak with the President. I also met Mrs. Clinton for the first time at this event. I did not get her autograph either. However, I made up for that later.

The First Lady of the United States

The Office of the First Lady is one of my favorite offices in the entire U.S. Government. The First Lady holds the most influential and most high profile, unelected position in our government. This has always been of great interest to me. I have worked hard at getting all of the living First Ladies' autographs. The toughest one to get is usually the autograph of a current First Lady.

A sitting First Lady receives thousands of letters on a variety of topics. It seems though that she does have a little more time to respond to autograph requests than does her husband. Still, it is mostly portraits of the First Lady with a facsimile or Autopened signature that are given to collectors.

My advice is to send something for the First Lady to sign, such as a magazine cover she is on, a book she has written, or just a book about First Ladies. If you mail the First Lady an item to autograph, she may feel more obligated to sign and send it back. The longer it takes to get a response, the better, because then you can be fairly assured that it has taken the First Lady that long to get through her other mail and authentically sign your item.

I have had two very positive experiences with First Lady Hillary Rodham Clinton. Immediately following the Inauguration, I sent Mrs. Clinton a copy of the January 1993 Good Housekeeping magazine to sign since she appeared on the cover. I sent it to the attention of her Social Secretary, Ann Stock, whom I saw on one of the morning news shows. About four months later, the magazine was sent back and it was personally signed: "To John....With Very Best Wishes....Hillary Rodham Clinton". I was ecstatic! I later heard that during those first few months in office, the Clintons set aside time just for the purpose of autographing items sent to them.

A little over a year later, I had the chance to get the First Lady's autograph in person. Mrs. Clinton and Mrs. Gore were co-hosting a dedication ceremony at The Vice President's Residence for a Native American sculpture, which was donated to The White House. The event took place about two weeks before I was to come home for the summer, so I knew it would be my last chance to get Mrs. Clinton's signature in person. I went prepared with her official portrait and one of my favorite black Sharpie Fine Point markers.

During the ceremony, Mrs. Gore and Mrs. Clinton were sitting together. Someone handed Mrs. Gore a program to sign and she handed it to Mrs. Clinton, who also signed it. As soon as the audience saw them sign the first program, they all rushed up afterward to get an autograph of their own. At this point, I thought for sure I would never get one, but I certainly was not going to miss this opportunity. I pulled out the picture and the Sharpie and I jumped in with the rest of the crowd.

As I approached Mrs. Clinton, she said she had to go and that the program she was signing would have to be her last. I was crushed. Mrs. Clinton's assistant, who was anxiously trying to move the First Lady along, told me to send the portrait to her and she would get it signed for me. I walked outside the tent and realized there had to be a way to get the First Lady's autograph. I told a nearby friend that I would ask Mrs. Clinton to sign the photo as she walked to her car, but that her assistant would probably hate me. My friend replied, "Do you really care if her assistant hates you?" That was all the encouragement I needed. As soon as Mrs. Clinton started toward her motorcade, I walked up to her and asked if she would please sign my picture "To John". The First Lady took the portrait and asked, "Is that J-o-n or J-o-h-n?" I now have a great remembrance of that day!

The Vice President of the United States

The Vice President's autograph is as tough to acquire as the President's signature. Once again, it is best to get an autograph in person if you are lucky enough to see the Vice President on the campaign trail or at a political event. Otherwise, you probably will receive a facsimile or staffer's forgery.

As an intern in Vice President Gore's Office, I had to work one morning a week in the mail room for the first four months of my internship. A book alone could be written about the type of mail a President and Vice President receives. It is amazing. I was fascinated by how some of the envelopes were addressed and the fact that they still made it to the right place.   A few had only "Vice President....White House" written on the envelope, but somehow they made it to the Vice President's mail room. Of course, I was most interested in the letters requesting autographs. A lot of people sent commemorative envelopes from the Inauguration for Vice President Gore to sign. Some people sent copies of his book, <u>Earth In The Balance</u>, which Al Gore wrote when he was a Senator from Tennessee.

My favorite story about getting the Vice President's autograph took place at a party I was helping with at The Vice President's Residence, which is located on the grounds of the U.S. Naval Observatory about twenty minutes from The White House. I was standing alone in the sun room when I saw Vice President Gore walk around the pool and stop to speak to a few people.

I quickly pulled out my invitation to the party and a Sharpie. No sooner did I do this then he walked through the door and there I was standing alone with the Vice President of the United States in his sun room. I shook his hand, reminded him that he had met me a few nights earlier, and then I asked him to sign my invitation, which he generously did. I have the signed invitation hanging behind my desk.

Later in the year, Mrs. Gore was gracious enough to have the Vice President sign a picture and a copy of his book for me! One of my most prized possessions is a signed picture of myself and the Vice President standing in his living room!

<u>The Second Lady of the United States</u>

The wife of the Vice President or Second Lady is the most accessible of the four main White House principals for autographs. During my eight months in Mrs. Tipper Gore's Office, I saw endless piles of pictures and other items to be signed. Mrs. Gore was so generous in fulfilling each and every request.

Few people even know who the Second Lady is at any given time and even fewer know that she works tirelessly for good causes and maintains a very important role at The White House. Immediately following the 1993 Inauguration, I wrote a long letter to Mrs. Gore telling her how much I admired her and how I thought she and the new Vice President looked like eternal high school sweethearts at the prom as they danced at one of the Inaugural Balls. Naturally, I requested an autographed picture. A few weeks later, I received an envelope from the Vice President's Office containing a signed picture of the Gores dancing. I wondered if the nature of the photo had anything to do with the subject of my letter. Little did I know then that I would be interning in Mrs. Gore's Office a few months later.

During my time with Mrs. Gore, I asked her to sign several items for me, including her official portrait, her book <u>Raising PG Kids In An X-Rated Society</u>, a Gore family portrait, a photo she had taken of the Vice President's Residence for its 100th Anniversary in 1993, and a picture of the two of us together in her office. These items along with my autographs from Al Gore are some of my most cherished mementos and they certainly highlight my collection.

The Children of the President and Vice President

Some people write to the children of the President and Vice President, known as the First and Second Families, respectively. My advice is to not even try to write the children for autographs, because you will not get one. You will most likely receive a polite form letter thanking you for writing and informing you that because the children are busy with school or other activities, they do not have time to respond to the public's requests.

The White House tries very hard to protect the First and Second Families' privacy, especially since the children did not ask to be put in that position. However, if you see the children in person and have the opportunity to get their signatures, then go for it. If you think about it, these children are in a club almost as exclusive as their parents' club.

Presidential Pets

Believe it or not, people do actually write to the President's pet. I believe it, because I am one of those people. I requested a "signed" photo of Socks, the Clintons' famous cat. Through connections, I finally received a picture of the Presidential kitty with an authentic paw print stamped at the bottom. This autograph is surely more rare than even the President's own signature.

It is definitely worth writing to pets just to see what you get in return. The Bush White House also sent out photos of their dog Millie, but after all, Millie had her own book in bookstores.

Former Presidents of the United States

Your best bet for getting a Presidential autograph is to write to the former Presidents. At this writing, there are four former, living Presidents: George Bush, Ronald Reagan, Jimmy Carter, and Gerald Ford. Each of the former Presidents has an office to which you can write them a letter. These men continue to receive large volumes of mail, especially autograph requests. If you write, you most likely will receive a portrait with a copy of their signature at the bottom.

Along with the photos I received of the former Presidents, they also enclosed a notecard thanking me for writing and explaining that because of the tremendous amount of mail they receive it is impossible for them to fulfill every request. In most cases, they feel it is unfair to choose among requests.

It is best if you send them something to sign. I sent Ronald Reagan, Jimmy Carter, and the late Richard Nixon copies of books they had written for them to autograph. Each of the books came back personally signed. I only paid $1.00 each for the Reagan and Nixon books and now they are worth considerably more than that.

I have written to Gerald Ford on several occasions and to a variety of different addresses and I have never received a reply. Once I even sent the letter to the attention of someone who I thought was one of his assistants.

I wrote President Nixon a couple of times and received no reply. Finally, I found the name of one of his assistants and sent the book to her attention. I received the signed book a couple of months before his death. I will treasure that autograph forever!

Several of the former Presidents have libraries named after them. If you cannot find an office address for a particular President, you should try sending your request to their Presidential Library.

Former First Ladies of the United States

Although former First Ladies receive a lot of mail, they seem willing and available to sign autographs. You should write to the First Ladies at their husbands' offices or libraries. In the case of Nancy Reagan, she has her own Foundation from which autographed pictures are sent.

I have received signed photos from all of the living, former First Ladies, except Lady Bird Johnson. My letters to Mrs. Johnson have received the reply that because of her age, Mrs. Johnson has had to stop autographing items. For this very reason, I wish I had started my collection long before I did. I have, however, received a Johnson family Christmas card and a photo from Mrs. Johnson sent via the L.B.J. Library. Therefore, my request was not a total loss.

Mrs. Reagan and Mrs. Bush seem to be the most willing to reply to autograph requests. I have written for and received three signed portraits and a signed memoir from Mrs. Reagan. Mrs. Bush generously sent me two signed pictures, signed copies of Millie's Book and Barbara Bush: A Memoir, two personally autographed book plates, and a handwritten note which in part congratulated me for graduating Summa Cum Laude from Marymount University.

It is interesting to note that I wrote to Mrs. Bush immediately following their return home to Houston in 1993 and I only received a bookmark and a generic note from the Office of George Bush. It pays to wait a few months until a former President and First Lady are settled into their new offices, because that is when I rewrote and received the signed items from Mrs. Bush.

In my first letter to Mrs. Carter, I invited her and her husband to my family's annual Fourth of July parade. I had invited several different celebrities in the hope of getting some sort of reply. Mrs. Carter's assistant wrote a nice letter back saying that the Carters were grateful for my invitation, but they had made other plans. Well of course they did, but I got the reply I wanted. Furthermore, she enclosed a notecard signed by Mrs. Carter. A year later, I wrote back and received a personally autographed portrait of Mrs. Carter, which I believe is a copy of her original White House portrait.

One of my biggest regrets in this genre is that I never got Jacqueline Kennedy Onassis' autograph. I wrote to her once at Doubleday Publishing where she worked as an Editor up until her death. I received a letter from the Editorial Department saying that Mrs. Onassis receives more requests for autographs than she can fulfill and she feels it would be inappropriate to choose among them. Although I was upset, I thought the response reflected Mrs. Onassis' great style. Even though I never did get Mrs. Onassis' signature, I did have the distinct honor of seeing her in person once.

I spent my 20th Birthday in Middleburg, Virginia, at the home of a friend and former freshman year roommate. One morning we went out to a fox hunt where my friend's father was riding. Mrs. Onassis was also there. Unfortunately, I did not get to meet her because she was already mounted on her white horse. I was content to just stand and watch her. To watch her was to watch history. With her death, the United States and, indeed, the world lost a most precious treasure.

Before Mrs. Onassis' death, I sent her a get-well card. Several months later I received a printed thank you note from John F. Kennedy, Jr. and Caroline Kennedy Schlossberg. I thought this was very thoughtful and showed a lot of class.

I hope to hang all of my portraits of First Ladies on my office wall someday!

To John Schlimm
With appreciation,
Al Gore

To John - Thanks for all your terrific
assistance -
Love, Tipper Gore

Top: Vice President Al Gore and I in HIS living room
Bottom: Tipper Gore and I in her office at the White House
White House Photographs

For John - with thanks from the Gore family - Tipper and Al Gore

To John - with love, Tipper Gore We miss you!

Top: A family portrait signed by the Vice President and Mrs. Gore
Photograph by Michael Evans
**Bottom: Mrs. Gore, my parents, my grandparents, and I at the
Vice President's Residence**
White House Photograph

**Here I am with two of my most admired ladies,
Sally Aman and Mrs. Gore**

I got this portrait of Hillary Rodham Clinton signed in person at the Vice President's Residence

BARBARA BUSH

9/30/94

Dear John Schimm –

Thank you for your kind letter about "A Memoir: Barbara Bush." I really loved writing the book, so hearing from people like you means a great deal to me. I have been lucky to share life with a remarkable man named George Bush and to be surrounded by family and great friends.

Thank you again for taking the time to write. George joins me in sending very best wishes to you and your family.

Thanks for your letter. Enclosed find a book plate to put in your book. Summa Cum Laude!! Great work! Congratulations! Barbara Bush

To John E. Schimm II
With best wishes
from

Ronald Reagan
Oct, 26 – '93

Top: A cherished note from Barbara Bush
Bottom Left: An inscription from Richard Nixon
Bottom Right: Ronald Reagan's signature

To John Schliwa
Best Wishes
Nancy Reagan

One of my favorite First Ladies, Nancy Reagan

Jimmy and Rosalynn Carter

To John - Best Wishes
Dan Quayle

To John   Best Wishes
Marilyn Quayle

Mondale

Joan Mondale

Top Left: Dan Quayle
Top Right: Marilyn Quayle
Bottom Left: Walter Mondale
Bottom Right: Joan Mondale

Top Left: Bill Bennett
Top Right: George Stephanopoulos
Bottom: James Brady

**Surely, this signature is even more rare than the president's autograph
An authentic pawprint from Socks, the Clintons' cat**

Former Vice Presidents of the United States

At the writing of this book, there are three former, living Vice Presidents: Dan Quayle, Walter Mondale, and Spiro Agnew. I have written to Mr. Agnew but have never received a reply. Apparently, he keeps a very low profile. I wrote to Walter Mondale a few years ago at his office in Minneapolis, Minnesota, and I received a signed notecard.

In the tradition of Washington recycling its politicians, former Vice President Mondale was appointed by President Clinton to serve as the U.S. Ambassador to Japan. I have written to him at that post, but I have yet to receive a reply.

I received a signed photo of former Vice President Dan Quayle right after he left office. For one of my college courses, I completed a large project based on Marilyn Quayle, which I will explain later. I sent the project to Mrs. Quayle along with portraits of Mrs. Quayle and her husband to be signed. A few weeks later, they both came back autographed. I later wrote to the Office of Dan Quayle in Indianapolis, Indiana, for another signed picture and I received his Official White House portrait with a facsimile of his signature. The night before my college graduation, I was fortunate enough to attend a book signing in McLean, Virginia, to promote Mr. Quayle's memoirs. I had him sign two copies; one was personally signed: "To John".

The thrill of writing to former Vice Presidents is not based only on the fact of who they once were, but that they tend to move on to other high profile positions after leaving the White House, such as running for President.

Former Second Ladies of the United States

Besides the Second Ladies who went on to be First Ladies, the wives of former Vice Presidents have done many things since leaving Washington. For example, Marilyn Quayle joined a prestigious law firm in Indianapolis. These women are little known American treasures whose autographs will surely highlight any collection.

I started writing to former Second Ladies when I found Mrs. Mondale's home address in Minneapolis. I sent my request to her directly. I later received a signed notecard, just like the one her husband had sent to me. When she moved to Japan after her husband's appointment as Ambassador, I wrote to her again. I have yet to receive a reply.

I have always been very fond of Mrs. Quayle. She worked hard to elevate the role of the Second Lady into an important and high profile position at The White House. During my sophomore year in college, I worked on an independent public relations project for which I created a fictional organization that Mrs. Quayle would found. My assignment was to complete all of the promotional materials and a public relations plan for the "Grand Opening" of the organization.

When I returned home for the summer, I wanted to send Mrs. Quayle a copy of the project. After the Quayles left Washington in 1993, Mrs. Quayle joined the prestigious law firm of Krieg DeVault Alexander & Capehart in Indianapolis. With a little research, I found the firm's address and sent the project to Mrs. Quayle along with portraits of Mrs. Quayle and her husband to be signed. A few weeks later, the pictures came back both personally signed by Mr. and Mrs. Quayle. Although I was thrilled, I was a bit disappointed that Mrs. Quayle did not even mention my project. At least I have the signed photos!

<u>Children of Former Presidents and Vice Presidents</u>

As I pointed out earlier, children of Presidents and Vice Presidents, current and former, are in an unique and exclusive club of their own. It can be fun to get autographs from these famous offsprings. It is a lot easier to get these signatures after the children leave the White House. Several of the children have gone on to other high profile positions.

John F. Kennedy, Jr. and Caroline Kennedy Schlossberg are the most famous Presidential children because of their high profile family; Steve Ford has been a television host; Patti Davis (Reagan) is the controversial author of several books about her life and other subjects; George W. Bush successfully ran for Governor of Texas in 1994; Lynda Johnson Robb is married to Chuck Robb, U.S. Senator from Virginia and former Governor; and Margaret Truman is the author of several murder mysteries set in Washington.

The only autographs from this genre that I have received are from Lynda Robb and Caroline Kennedy. I wrote to Mrs. Robb's husband's Senate Office for her picture and I attended a lecture Caroline Kenndy gave at George Washington University to get her new book signed. Otherwise, addresses for these people can be very difficult to find.

Current and Former White House Staffers

The White House is a treasure chest of autographs waiting to be discovered. Not only are the four principals' autographs worth seeking, but so are the signatures of many current and former White House staff members. Many people who work and who have worked in the Executive Branch of the U.S. Government have become celebrities in their own right, whether it is because of their high profile position or something they did. This group includes Press Secretaries, Top Aides, Advisors, Chiefs of Staff, etc...

Most everyone who has worked in a high profile position at The White House has gone on to work in other important jobs. I discovered this upon doing another college project. During my senior year in college, I researched White House Press Secretaries to First and Second Ladies for my final Communications paper. As part of my research, I wrote to all the living, current and former White House Press Secretaries. I asked each one of them to send me a signed picture and a letter explaining what they personally felt about their role as a Press Secretary to a President or First Lady.

Since I worked side-by-side with Tipper Gore's Press Secretary, Sally Aman, I was afforded an unique look at the job. Sally is the first Press Secretary to serve a Vice President's wife and she is by far the best at her job!

The response I received from the former Press Secretaries was overwhelming to me. Almost everyone I had written responded in one way or another. I received autographed photos and very personal letters. George Reedy, former Press Secretary to President Johnson, wrote in his letter: "The true objective of the job is to foster communication between the President and the American people. This means that the press must have absolute confidence that the Press Secretary is speaking the truth whenever he opens his mouth"; Ronald L. Ziegler, former Press Secretary to President Nixon, wrote: "Among the lessons I learned from my tenure as Press Secretary is one from President Nixon himself. In the midst of a trying time in American history, the President used his mind in a disciplined manner"; Rosalynn Carter's former Press Secretary, Mary Finch Hoyt, sent me her phone number if I had any questions; and Lady Bird Johnson's former Press Secretary, Liz Carpenter, sent me a personally signed copy of her book. The letters were most helpful and I went on to write an "A" paper.

Other former White House staffers to whom I have written include Letitia Baldridge, who was Jacqueline Kennedy's Social Secretary, and Don Regan, who was Ronald Reagan's Chief of Staff for a period of time. Members of the Clinton Administration whom I have written include Mack McLarty, Leon Panetta, Dee Dee Myers, and George Stephanopoulos.

It is fun to see these men and women on television every day and be able to write to them. Even though they really have become well-known because of their close proximity to the President, a few of them have come from other top government jobs. For example, Mr. Panetta is a former Congressman from California.

It is easy to reach current White House staffers because you can write to them at The White House. To write former staffers, you may have to do a little research to find out where they are now. One of the Press Secretaries to whom I did not write was Anna Perez, former Press Secretary to Barbara Bush, because I could not find out where she was working. A few months later while reading Mrs. Bush's memoirs, I learned that Ms. Perez was working at Creative Artists Agency in Los Angeles.

The President's Cabinet

The President's Cabinet is made up of the appointed Secretaries of the Departments of State, Treasury, Interior, Agriculture, Justice, Commerce, Labor, Defense, Housing and Urban Development, Transportation, Energy, Education, Health and Human Services, and Veteran's Affairs. These men and women are very high profile officials and have come from a variety of backgrounds, some political, others not. I have written to all of President Clinton's Cabinet Secretaries, but only one sent an authentic autograph. The rest appear to be Autopen signatures. Some Cabinet members will enclose form letters saying that because of the demand, they cannot personally sign their pictures.

I did get one Cabinet member's autograph in person. I went to the 1994 Easter Egg Role at The White House. Since I knew there would be several notable figures there, I took a portrait of The White House to have them all sign. As I was walking through the Ellipse, I noticed Attorney General Janet Reno and her security guard walking about twenty feet in front of me. No one seemed to recognize her, which I found strange since she is so tall and has such defining features. I immediately ran over to her and asked her to sign my picture, which she kindly did. I am proud to take credit for the clutch that soon surrounded her. She spent the next thirty minutes signing autographs and having her picture taken with fans.

It is a lot easier to get autographs from former Cabinet members, who usually move on to other jobs, either in the government or the private sector. One of my favorite former Cabinet Secretaries is Elizabeth Dole, wife of Senator Bob Dole from Kansas. Mrs. Dole served as the Secretary of Transportation under

President Ronald Reagan and went on to be the Secretary of Labor under President George Bush. After resigning her post at The Department of Labor, Mrs. Dole became the President of the American Red Cross.

I have written to Mrs. Dole on two occasions and each time I received great responses. First, I received a letter with a handwritten note at the bottom. Next, I received Mrs. Dole's portrait. The note on the portrait reads in part: "With many thanks for your fine work on behalf of others and your very kind comments."

Other former Cabinet members whose autographs I have acquired include former Labor Secretary Lynn Martin, whom I met at a political fundraiser, former Defense Secretary Dick Cheney, former Defense Secretary Casper Weinberger, former Secretary of Housing and Urban Development Jack Kemp, and former Education Secretary Bill Bennett.

I had several reasons for writing to some of these people. Jack Kemp, Bill Bennett, Dick Cheney, and Lynn Martin may all run for President. Elizabeth Dole could be a future First Lady or perhaps even Vice President! I have also written to Joanne Kemp, wife of Jack Kemp, who may also be a prospective First Lady.

I do have a story about Lynn Martin. I met her at a fundraiser at a house in Arlington, Virginia. After I had my picture taken with her, I realized I did not have anything for her to sign. While she was speaking, I snuck away and started going through drawers trying to find a notecard or anything Ms. Martin could autograph. I even had the housekeeper helping me, so I did not feel too guilty. Finally, I found a notecard and I handed it, along with specific instructions, to the girl who was driving Ms. Martin back to the airport. About a hour later, I had my authentically signed notecard.

You can also write to the Deputy Secretaries if you are really interested in this genre. Sometimes, one of these people will become controversial. For example, I wrote to then Deputy Treasury Secretary Roger Altman, who resigned amidst controversy during the Whitewater hearings. I received a typed thank you note for my interest and it was signed by Mr. Altman.

CHAPTER 2
THE LEGISLATIVE BRANCH

Senators of the United States

The Senate of the United States offers a wide range of possibilities for an autograph collector. One hundred men and women, two from each state, make up this half of the Legislative Branch of Government. Each Senator has offices both in Washington and in their home state. A Senator's office is not in the actual Capitol building, but is located in a scattering of buildings surrounding the Capitol. These buildings are Russell, Dirksen, and Hart.

Since Senatorial elections are held every six years with one third of the Senate seats up for election each time, this genre of autograph collecting frequently changes faces and possibilities.

It is best to send autograph requests to a particular Senator's office on Capitol Hill. For a list of exact addresses for each Senator, you should call the Capitol or your Senator's Office.

If you do not care to write to all of the Senators, focus on writing to the more well-known Senators, who may move on to even higher political positions. After all, both Dan Quayle and Al Gore were Members of the House of Representatives and resided in the Senate before they were elected Vice President of the United States.

I have written to all one hundred Senators several times each and I still do not have all of their pictures. I do have a few interesting stories about my experiences writing to Senators that I would like to share with you.

Some Senators send you a picture immediately and others seem to take forever. Senators have huge staffs with various people handling such requests, so it is a reflection on the Senator's staff as to how long it takes to get a reply and what kind of reply you finally receive. The autographs I tend to remember the most are the ones that were the toughest to get. In a lot of offices, authorized staff members sign their boss' signature. Once again, my policy is to just not think about it and enjoy what I receive.

Two of the most difficult autographed portraits for me to obtain are from Senator Bob Dole of Kansas and Senator Ted Kennedy of Massachusetts. I wrote to each of these men several times, but received no reply. Finally, I wrote and said how much I like their states and that perhaps I would move there one day. I certainly do not advise lying, but, unfortunately, sometimes it is the only way to get a response from these offices. And it must have worked, because within a few

To John
With best wishes,

Bob Dole

Bob Dole

To John - With many thanks for your kind words and all best wishes,
Elizabeth Dole

One of my favorite political spouses, Elizabeth Dole

weeks, I received signed portraits from both of them. I had a similar problem when getting former Senator Harris Wofford's portrait and my home is in the state he represented, Pennsylvania.

I had a strange experience when writing to Senator Larry Craig's Office. One day I received a phone call from someone in his office and I was told that because they were trying to cut down on costs around the office, Senator Craig of Idaho could not send me a picture. The first thing I wondered was how much the phone call cost, especially since I live in northwestern Pennsylvania. I later solved the problem by writing to Senator Craig again and this time I enclosed a Self-Addressed, Stamped Envelope (S.A.S.E.). This is usually unnecessary since Senators have the Franking Privilege. I received a signed photo a few weeks later.

A little known treasure of the U.S. Senate is former astronaut, Senator John Glenn of Ohio. His photograph, a portrait of him as an astronaut, was one of the first and most thrilling autographs I received. He is definitely someone to whom you should write whether or not you are collecting portraits of all the Senators.

Another fun project and one, of course, I am fond of is writing to the spouses of these men and women. Some of these spouses are well-known in their own right. You should always keep in the back of your mind that one of these Senators and their spouse could make it to The White House someday. For example, Marilyn Quayle and Tipper Gore were once spouses of the Senate. Currently, some of the more well known Senatorial spouses include Lynda Johnson Robb and Elizabeth Dole, both of whom have sent me signed pictures.

You can write to spouses of Senators by sending the letters directly to the Senator's office in Washington or one of their offices in their home state, especially since many spouses spend a lot of time in their home state because of family or other jobs. If you do a little research about these spouses, you will find that many of them do some extraordinary things, such as working tirelessly for various charities or carrying on with careers of their own.

I had the pleasure of seeing and meeting a lot of these spouses when I volunteered at a Congressional Spouses Healthcare Briefing that Mrs. Clinton and Mrs. Gore co-hosted on Capitol Hill. Another volunteer and I were in charge of handing out some of the name tags to spouses.

Before the spouses arrived, the other volunteer and I discussed the polished "look" some politicians and spouses have that puts them in a special category. You cannot really explain the "look", but you sure know it when you see it. So as each of the spouses, mostly women, came in, we analyzed them as to if they had the "look" or not. I was truly amazed that political spouses come in all shapes, sizes, and ages.

The spouse who made the biggest impression on me and one who definitely has the "look" is Vicki Kennedy, Senator Ted Kennedy's wife. She is tall, young, and beautiful. And to top it off, she is a lawyer. I truly wanted to meet Mrs. Kennedy, but I had to choose between meeting her or having my picture taken with First Lady Hillary Rodham Clinton. I will let you guess which one I chose!

United States House of Representatives

The Congress of the United States is made up of 435 Members, all representing various districts back in their home states. The House also includes five delegates who represent the District of Columbia, Guam, Puerto Rico, America Samoa, and the Virgin Islands. These Members of the other half of the Legislative Branch of Government offer a true smorgasbord of backgrounds, ages, ethnic groups, and interests. Since elections for Members of Congress are held every two years with all of the House seats up for election, it would be almost impossible to write to all of the Members, unless you totally focused on just this genre. There are, however, some better known Members of the House who are excellent prospects for autograph seekers.

It can be fun to write to your own Member of Congress, whether or not he or she is very famous. The members you want to write to otherwise should be ones that you know will move on to higher offices, such as Senator or Governor and in some cases, even President or Vice President. These are the men and women to whom I have chosen to write letters. Like the Senate Office Buildings, office buildings for House Members are also scattered about on Capitol Hill. The House Office Buildings are Rayburn, Longworth, Cannon, Annex 1- O'Neill, and Annex 2- Ford.

I wrote to my own Congressman, Bill Clinger of Pennsylvania. I also wrote to Tom Foley of Washington, former Speaker of the House; Newt Gingrich of Georgia, current Speaker of the House and potential candidate for President; Tom Ridge of Pennsylvania, who successfully ran for Governor in 1994; Dick Armey of Texas, a potential candidate for President; Bob Dornan of California, one of the more outspoken members of the Republican Party; Fred Grandy of Iowa, former Gubernatorial candidate and Gofer on The Love Boat; Dan Rostenkowski of Illinois, former Congressman and a controversial figure in the House and Senate banking scandal; Rick Santorum of Pennsylvania, who successfully ran against Harris Wofford for his Senate seat in 1994; and Leslie Byrne of Virginia, who makes it a point to authentically sign every autograph request she receives.

These men and women are really the grass roots politicians in Washington, because they represent smaller areas than Senators and can be a strong voice for their constituents. During campaign seasons, these Representatives are fairly easy to meet at political events. If you do get to meet one of them, be sure to get an autograph.

For a detailed list of all the Members of the House of Representatives and their addresses, you can call or write to your local Member's office or the U.S. Capitol.

Remember that you can also write to the spouses of House Members. You never know which one might be the next First or Second Lady or next husband of a Governor.

If you have an inkling someone may go on to a higher office, it might be fun to write them and say something like: "I know you will be a First Lady someday and you will be wonderful in that role. Will you please send me your personalized autograph?"

Newt Gingrich

CHAPTER 3
THE JUDICIAL BRANCH

Supreme Court Justices of the United States

There are nine members of the Supreme Court of the United States. The Judicial Branch of our Government includes a Chief Justice and eight Associate Justices. Although an appointment to the Supreme Court is for life, there are a few retired Justices still alive. All of the Justices can be reached by writing to them at The Supreme Court of the United States in Washington.

I first wrote to all of the Justices while doing a graphology project, which is the study of handwriting. I received nice responses as several of them replied with autographed cards, which were embossed with their name and the seal of The Supreme Court of the United States.

I later wrote for all of their pictures. This time, a few new Justices responded to my request. The pictures, like the notecards, are all done in the same style, which would make a nice display if you were to frame and hang them.

One thing I did learn on both writings was that Justice Antonin Scalia will not send his autograph in response to mail requests. This upset me a little, because during my freshman year at Marymount University, Justice Scalia came and spoke as part of a Speaker's Series and I had met him. I did not collect autographs at the time, so I did not ask him for his signature. I will always regret missing out on that one.

I have not had much luck with writing to the retired Justices. I imagine that when they retired, they also retired from answering the huge volumes of mail and autograph requests. Who can blame them?

I did get signed photos of Justices Byron White and Harry Blackmun before they retired. I have yet to receive photos from their successors, Justices Ruth Bader Ginsburg and Stephen Breyer. Justice Ginsburg is an important figure because she is the second woman to be added to the Supreme Court; Justice Sandra Day O'Connor was the first.

Justice Clarence Thomas is one of the better known members of the Supreme Court because of the controversy he encountered over the Anita Hill sexual harassment case during his confirmation hearings. He is the second African American to be added to the court; the late Justice Thurgood Marshall was the first.

Since there are only nine Justices, it may seem easy to get all of their autographs, but that is not true. It helps to be patient and to write several times.

To John Schlimm —
I wish you all the best!
Clarence Thomas

Justice Clarence Thomas

Supreme Court of the United States
Washington, D. C. 20543

CHAMBERS OF
THE CHIEF JUSTICE

[signature: William H. Rehnquist]

Supreme Court of the United States
Washington, D. C. 20543

CHAMBERS OF
JUSTICE SANDRA DAY O'CONNOR

[signature: Sandra Day O'Connor]

Supreme Court of the United States
Washington, D. C. 20543

CHAMBERS OF
JUSTICE BYRON R. WHITE

[signature: Byron White]

Supreme Court of the United States
Washington, D. C. 20543

CHAMBERS OF
JUSTICE DAVID H. SOUTER

[signature: David Souter]

Top Left: Chief Justice William H. Rehnquist
Top Right: Justice Sandra Day O'Connor
Bottom Left: Retired Justice Byron R. White
Bottom Right: Justice David H. Souter

CHAPTER 4
STATE AND LOCAL OFFICIALS

<u>Governors of the United States</u>

The Governors of the United States make up a fascinating genre of autograph collecting. Each state has a Governor who usually lives in the Governor's Mansion in the capital of the state he represents and has a working office in the State Capitol Building. These men and women represent every facet of politics and political success stories imaginable: Some have risen from poverty and slowly climbed the political ladder; others are millionaires who have served a proud tradition of getting elected to office; and still others have gone on to be the President of the United States.

I have written to all 50 Governors and a few former Governors. Since there are Gubernatorial elections held somewhere in the United States every year, it has been hard at times to know who exactly is still Governor and of which state. Often, I have written and simply addressed the letter to "The Governor" and then wrote the capital and state to which I was sending the letter. The letters always seem to get there and when the Governors reply, I learn their names. You can, however, get a list of Governors and their addresses by calling your local Representative's office or State Capitol.

The responses I have received from Governors vary: I have received big pictures and little pictures, signed photos and unsigned photos, postcards, bumper stickers, letters, and even a few embarrassing notes informing me that the person to whom I wrote is no longer Governor!

As with any political genre of autographs, you should aim for those who might move on to other high political posts. For example, President Clinton was once the Governor of Arkansas and President Reagan was once the Governor of California. I have written to some Governors because I believe they will run for The White House someday. These Governors are George Allen of Virginia, of whom I have several stories to tell later, Christine Todd Whitman of New Jersey, Jim Edgar of Illinois, Evan Bayh of Indiana, Carroll Campbell of South Carolina, and Pete Wilson of California. Time will only tell what these fine politicians will do next in their political careers.

I wrote to Governor Robert Casey of Pennsylvania in 1993. I do regret having missed the chance to meet Governor Casey when St. Marys was "Capital For A Day". I encourage everyone to at least write to the Governor of their home state.

Governors have several items that they can send out to autograph collectors. I know this because I have written to one of my favorite Governors, Jim Edgar, and his wife several times. Often, it pays to mail your request to the First Lady of a state, who may be a more direct contact for you to the Governor. Governor Edgar has sent me two signed portraits, a signed picture of him and his wife, who bares a striking resemblance to a young Jackie Kennedy, and a signed notecard with his name embossed on the top.

Two of my more notable autographs are from the late Governor George Mickelson of South Dakota, who was killed in a plane crash on the same day I received his autograph, and Governor Guy Hunt of Alabama, whose autograph I received during the same week he was forced to resign because of alleged violations.

You can even write to former Governors of states who often go on to do other remarkable things. Your letters to these men and women can be sent to their State Capitol where they will then be forwarded to the appropriate address.

The only Governor I have ever met and known is Governor George Allen of Virginia. I had several opportunities to meet and talk with him during his campaign because I attended college in Arlington, Virginia, and my friend Roland volunteered for the Allen campaign. I will share some of my stories about George and Susan Allen later when I discuss getting autographs from candidates. I probably have more Allen autographs than anyone else, even in Virginia.

First Ladies of the States

For the sake of all the wonderful female Governors we have and those Governors who are not married, let me just say that there are more wives of Governors than there are husbands or single Governors, and because of my interest in First Ladies, I have especially enjoyed writing to Governors' wives all over the United States. Many people may not even know that the wife of a Governor is called the First Lady of the state. The husbands of Governors have no title, official or unofficial, yet and I suspect they will not get one until the United States labels the first husband of a President or Vice President.

As a great admirer of the First Ladies of the United States, I was thrilled to learn that almost all the states have First Ladies. This opened up a whole new genre and interest for me.

I was able to find the names of the Governors' spouses by looking in The Almanac of American Politics. This is a wonderful source book, which is updated every two years and lists all the major politicians, nationally and locally, gives short biographies on each, and lists their addresses. This book is helpful for any genre of political autographs and can usually be found at your local library or bookstore.

After obtaining my list of names, I sent the letters to the State Capitols. Usually, First Ladies have their own offices, either at the State Capitol or at the Governor's Mansion. First Ladies take on extraordinary causes and travel their state promoting these causes. Some of the spouses of Governors have careers of their own. These women are as admirable as their husbands. When writing these women, be sure to also ask for a copy of their biographies. You will surely be impressed with what a lot of them have done. The growing importance of the roles these women play in their state and in their husbands' political careers is no doubt a direct reflection of the growing and increasingly significant role that the First and Second Ladies of the United States have in their husbands' administrations.

When I first started writing to Governors' wives, I asked them for samples of their handwriting for my graphology project. Some First Ladies, such as Brenda Edgar of Illinois, sent wonderful replies. Other First Ladies wrote letters claiming it was inappropriate or a security risk for them to send a sample of their handwriting. Some of these letters even bordered on stuck-up. One First Lady wrote: "I know you must be very excited about the possibility of analyzing my handwriting and signature, but for security reasons this is not something we can share." I was not that excited!

My reaction to these negative letters was to write again and only ask for an autographed picture. Almost all of them sent me one.

I do have a few favorite former and current First Ladies of states and I tend to write them often for different pictures. These women include Brenda Edgar, Susan Bayh of Indiana, Ellen Casey of Pennsylvania, Phyllis George of Kentucky, and Susan Allen of Virginia, whom I count as a friend and whom I will tell stories about in the "Candidate" section of this book.

State and Local Government Officials

Your own state and hometown governments are great places from which to get autographs. Autographs that you can collect include signatures from the Lieutenant Governor, Spouse of the Lieutenant Governor, State Attorney General, State Treasurer, State Supreme Court Justices, State Senators, State Representatives, and even the mayor of your own hometown. Writing to these people can be a great and fun lesson about how your state operates and who runs it. This could be especially exciting for a class to do as a group or individual project.

I have written mostly to officials in my home state of Pennsylvania. I have received autographed portraits from the Lieutenant Governor and his wife, the state Attorney General, the state Treasurer, my local state Representative, and my state Senator. The most endearing autographed picture came from the mayor of my small town, St. Marys. I have known Mayor Anne Grosser for several years.

Mayor Grosser is a wonderful and witty lady. I was not even sure if she would have a picture to send out, but a few days after I wrote to her I received this envelope with a small, autographed picture of Anne standing by one of her campaign signs. She also sent a personal letter, which I suspect she typed herself. It was so heartwarming. I hope she is our Mayor for many years to come!

I have written to a few out-of-state local officials, whom I believe will go on to have very promising careers in politics. When I first met Bret Schundler, Mayor of Jersey City, New Jersey, I was told that after the tough election he had recently won, he was one of the stars of the Republican Party. I did not have to be told anymore than that. Before I attended the fundraiser at which he was appearing, I called his office in Jersey City and said that I was doing a project on American Mayors. I realize it was a little white lie, but they would not have sent me the unsigned photo otherwise. I received the photo a day before the event and off I went with Roland and some of his other Republican buddies, who got me into the event for free. I also took my camera and had my picture taken with Mayor Schundler, which I later sent to him to sign. He was rather surprised when I presented his portrait for him to autograph. He asked me where I got it. I responded, "Your office sent it to me."

The best part of this story occurred when I wrote to his wife, Lynn Schundler, the First Lady of Jersey City. I figured, if Bret Schundler is going places politically, then so is his wife. I wrote Mrs. Schundler a long letter telling her how wonderful she is and what a terrific First Lady she would be if Bret ever makes it to The White House. Several weeks later I received a handwritten letter from Mrs. Schundler. It reads in part: "I'm not sure if you were serious, but I'll assume you were! Thank you. Your letter certainly made my day! Enclosed is the requested autographed picture." It is one of the favorite items in my collection. Just think how treasured it will be if the Schundlers ever do make it to The White House.

Christine Todd Whitman of New Jersey

To John Schlimm -
a great guy and valued
friend!
Keep smiling always,
Mayor Anne Grosser
6/25/94

To: John

Best Regards -

Jim + Brenda
Edgar

**Top: Writing to local politicians can be fun. Here is a picture and
inscription from my hometown Mayor, Anne Grosser.
Bottom: Jim and Brenda Edgar of Illinois**

CHAPTER 5
CANDIDATES

Candidates are the most accessible political figures from whom to get autographs, though in some cases you have to use a little logic, be forward, and have a great sense of adventure. Almost every year is an election year for some government officials. The biggest campaigns are for President and Vice President, U.S. Senator, U.S. Representative, Governor, Lieutenant Governor, and State Attorney General. There are also numerous elections for other state and local positions, which can be very exciting. Candidates and their spouses are constantly traveling and trying to meet as many people as possible, which includes attending numerous events, both public and private.

You can usually find out what a candidate's schedule is by either calling the candidate's campaign headquarters or by asking someone at your local party headquarters.

When you are attending an event, you should be organized and ready to get an autograph. Candidates usually are surrounded by other supporters who want to talk with them and also get their autograph. A candidate's staff members may try to keep the candidate moving along through a huge group. For this reason, you have to be prepared to get the autograph.

First, you should have something for the candidate and/or a spouse to sign. This item could be any number of things, including a portrait of the candidate or candidate's family, campaign literature, a campaign poster (my favorite), a bumper sticker, a book the candidate has written, a news article about the candidate, or anything else that has the candidate's name on it. Other items candidates will likely sign include American or state flags, copies of the U.S. Constitution, T-shirts, state maps, and notecards.

When getting a candidate's autograph in person, the candidate will most likely be friendly and usually willing to sign since they are trying to please as many people as possible.

It is next to impossible to receive a candidate's autograph by writing to their campaign headquarters, which receives a huge abundance of mail.

Another possibility is to wait until after the election and then write to the candidate who lost. Usually, the losing candidate goes on to run for another office in the future or works in the private sector. The candidates in this category you should focus on are former Presidential and Vice Presidential Candidates. You can send them books and campaign literature to sign or they usually have portraits they will sign and send back to you.

During my last year in college, there were several campaigns occurring in

Virginia. I have many fond memories from these times, which I usually shared with my friend Roland. At many political events, we were partners in crime! One of us would take the picture while the other was posing with a candidate or political spouse and securing an autograph and then we would switch. I always used a Sharpie Fine Point marker and we always asked for two pictures with the candidate in case one did not turn out, which happened quite often.

During 1994, Oliver North unsuccessfully ran for Senator Chuck Robb's U.S. Senate seat in Virginia. Since several of his events were held close to Arlington, Roland and I would race from place to place to get his autograph. One day, we went to three separate events. I do not even think Mr. North knew us from one event to the next. At the various events, I had Mr. North sign copies of his two books, a campaign sign, and several pieces of campaign literature. It got to the point, I ran out of items for him to sign and, frankly, I was a little tired of seeing him. I also had his wife, Betsy, sign one of the books. She wrote the date in the book below her name because she said she likes to look back to see when she received a signed book and she thought maybe I would as well.

My most vivid memories from this genre are from the 1993 Gubernatorial campaign in Virginia. Former Congressman George Allen successfully ran against Virginia's Attorney General Mary Sue Terry to become the 67th Governor of the Commonwealth of Virginia. In January of 1993, I attended a house party for George and Susan Allen. I immediately fell in love with the couple. They are young, smart, and they definitely have the "look". As usual, I was more concerned with the spouse than the actual candidate. I believe that a candidate and a spouse are more of a team running than just one person.

After getting Mr. Allen's first of many autographs, Roland and I practically pulled Susan Allen into the dining room where we were awed by her charm. I told her that I love First Ladies and how she would be one of the best. I then had my picture taken with her and had her sign the same piece of campaign literature her husband had just autographed for me.

I did not see the Allens for several months because I went home for summer vacation. However, when I went back to college, I started attending political events again with Roland, who had spent the summer in Arlington working for the Arlington County Republican Committee. One day, I went to a Metro stop in Virginia to have George sign another piece of campaign literature. Then, the Republican Party of Virginia debuted this great and colorful campaign poster with the names of the three major candidates: George Allen for Governor, Mike Farris for Lieutenant Governor, and James Gilmore III for Attorney General. This poster presented a new challenge: Could I get all three candidates to sign it? Roland and I set out attending a very early morning breakfast to get Jim Gilmore's autograph, a Sunday morning breakfast to get Mike Farris'

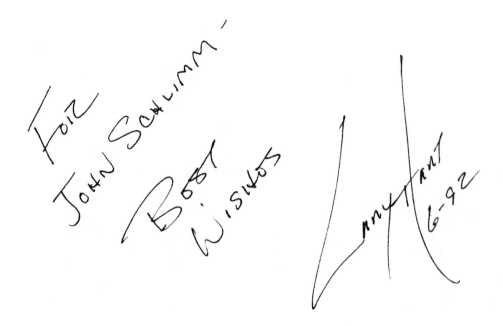

For
John Schumm -
Best Wishes
Gary Hart
6-92

Oliver North for
U.S. Senate Committee

P.O. Box 10851
Chantilly, VA 22021
(703) 802-6600
FAX: (703) 802-6607

John —
Oliver North

Top: Gary Hart, who ran for President in 1984 and 1988
Bottom: Oliver North, who ran for the U.S. Senate in 1994

Top: Governor George Allen and I during the 1993 gubernatorial race
Bottom: Susan Allen and I after I first met her
Photographs by Roland R. Foster

signature, and we even volunteered at a fundraiser so we could get in to have George Allen sign the poster. I bet that we are the only two people in Virginia who have this poster signed by all three candidates!

These events presented many comical moments. At the Gilmore breakfast, Roland and I were holding our posters, in fact we were the only two holding posters, and someone walked up to us and said, "Are you going to hang those up or just carry them around all day?" In unison, we replied, "Carry them around all day!" At the Farris breakfast, his opponent, Lieutenant Governor Don Beyer and his wife were also there, so I set out to get Mrs. Beyer's autograph. My one problem was that I did not know what she looked like. I walked up to one lady and asked her if she could point out Mrs. Beyer to me. She replied, "I'm Mrs. Beyer!"

During two months of events, I always missed seeing Susan Allen. Finally, we heard that she was going to be campaigning at the Metro stop by our townhouse. Armed with a camera, a Sharpie, and the January photo of us together, I set out for the Metro. As Roland and I walked up to the future First Lady of Virginia, I said, "Susan, I'm not sure if you remember us..." Without another word, Susan replied, "I remember you two, I met you both back in January at Robert Baratta's house." I was struck speechless. I could not believe she remembered us after ten months. We became her two biggest fans! I had her sign my picture and I had a new photo taken with her. I asked her to sign the photo "From Your Favorite First Lady...", but she replied that she could not because she was not the First Lady of Virginia yet. I later wrote to her after the election and she sent me her portrait with that inscription.

We saw George and Susan a few more times over the next few weeks as the election drew near. I had two more items for George to sign, so we set out at 5:00 A.M. one morning to greet him at a Metro stop about twenty-five minutes from our townhouse. When we got there, he was campaigning with Jim Gilmore and Susan. I went up to George and asked him to sign a blue and white "Allen for Governor" poster in red and the picture of the two of us in black. He seemed a bit taken aback by my specific request, but kindly obliged. In between signing, he tried to introduce me to the future Attorney General. I said I had already met him and sort of brushed him aside. I hope I was not too rude but I become very territorial when seeking autographs. Besides, I already had gotten Mr. Gilmore's autograph. I also had Susan sign the "Allen" poster.

The most cinematic moment of this campaign occurred when we attended an "Allen" Rally a few days before the election. Roland and I had a picture of the two of us and Susan blown-up and framed. We signed the picture: "To Susan....Our Favorite First Lady....From Your Two Biggest Fans....Love Roland....Love John". After the rally, the crowd mobbed the Allens, but we eventually found our way to Susan. We gave her the picture and she hugged us. Then, as she was about to get in the car to leave, she turned, caught our eyes, and said, "See you later guys!" We yelled back, "We love you Susan!"

I feel so lucky to know Susan Allen. I know she and her husband will live in The White House someday!

While interning at The White House, I ran into Kathleen Brown, who at the time was running for Governor of California. I was sitting in the cafeteria with some other interns when I recognized Kathleen from across the room. Two of the interns who were from California did not even know whom she was. I sprinted back to Mrs. Gore's Office to get paper and a pen and then I rushed back to the cafeteria. I approached Ms. Brown and asked for her autograph, which she gave to me. Whenever I got autographs at The White House, I would have the celebrity sign a piece of the Vice President's stationery so I would have a keepsake of where I got the autograph. I have several of these sheets signed by various notable figures.

Former Presidential and Vice Presidential candidates can be very exciting people to whom to write for autographs. Regardless of the fact they lost, they still made a significant impression in the history of the United States. I have written to a few of the more notable, former candidates including Barry Goldwater, who ran for President in 1964; Gary Hart, who ran for President in 1984 and 1988; Michael and Kitty Dukakis, who ran for The White House in 1988; Paul Tsongas, who ran for President in 1992; and Geraldine Ferraro, who made history in 1984 as the first woman to run for Vice President of the United States. There are several officials in other elected positions who have run for President and whom I will not mention here, but I have most of their autographs and have already discussed them.

When I wrote to Admiral James Stockdale, who was Ross Perot's Vice Presidential running mate in 1992, for a sample of his handwriting, he responded with a personal, handwritten letter, which reads in part: "As you can see, my handwriting in its 'relaxed' form is an odd combination of script and printing. It drives my wife Sybil, who is an excellent scribe with beautiful script, nuts."

Out of all these people, Geraldine Ferraro's autograph has become one of the most difficult to acquire. When I first wrote to her, she sent a signed notecard. When I later wrote, I received a letter saying that I would only receive a signed portrait of Ms. Ferraro if I donated money to a scholarship fund in her mother's name. I am content with the signed notecard!

As for future Presidential candidates, it is widely known that a Presidential campaign unofficially begins the day after the last Inauguration. From that time on, there is much speculation as to whom will run in the next Presidential election. There is no better time to write to the prospective candidates than as soon as you hear their names mentioned. As time goes on, they will become busier and may not have time to fulfill autograph requests. And, should they reside in The White House someday, their signature will be next to impossible to get!

Geraldine Ferraro

CHAPTER 6
U.S. MILITARY LEADERS

The highest military leader in the United States is The President, who is the Commander-in-Chief of the Armed Forces. The President, along with the National Security Council and Secretary of Defense, are directly advised by the Joint Chiefs of Staff. The Joint Chiefs of Staff are made up of the Chairman of the Joint Chiefs of Staff, Chief of Staff of the U.S. Army, Chief of Naval Operations, Chief of Staff of the U.S. Air Force, and the Commandant of the Marine Corps. There is also the Vice Chairman of the Joint Chiefs of Staff and the Commandant of the U.S. Coast Guard from whom you can request an autograph.

I have written to all of these leaders and have received a response from each one. Some of them personally signed their photo "To John", others just signed their name, and one or two do not sign official portraits. The Joint Chiefs of Staff can all be reached at The Pentagon in Arlington, Virginia.

The most well known and former Chairman of the Joint Chiefs of Staff is Retired General Colin Powell. I originally wrote to him for my graphology project and he sent back a signed letter and a little signed card. While he was still Chairman, I wrote for a signed portrait, which I received. After he retired, I wrote to him again. This time, I received another signed portrait. I am especially interested in General Powell because he may run for office someday, perhaps even the Presidency. Because of this, I also wrote to his wife, Alma Powell, a prospective First Lady.

Mrs. Powell responded with a charming and, to my delight, handwritten note explaining that she has no photos of herself to send out but that she hoped the note would suffice. It sure did!

I found out the names of the Chiefs of Staff by asking some friends who are interested in the military and by doing some research on my own. You can also call The Pentagon for a list of these officials.

I am fortunate in that a former member of the Joint Chiefs of Staff is from my hometown. Former Army Chief of Staff General Edward C. Meyer was born and raised in St. Marys, Pennsylvania. As a town, we are immensely proud our own native son. St. Marys even has a "General Edward Meyer Boulevard" running through town. I have had the honor of meeting General Meyer and I received his autograph when I was very young.

Throughout history, there have been many fine and notable military figures. One notable military figure in recent years is Retired General H. Norman Schwarzkopf. During Desert Storm, "Storm'in" Norman became a great military hero and a national treasure. I originally wrote to him and invited him and his family to join us for our annual Fourth of July parade. As with the Carters, I did not expect him to come, but I was curious as to what response I would get. He sent a nice letter thanking me for the invitation, but wrote that he and his son, Christian, were going salmon fishing in Alaska over the holiday. I later wrote to him and asked for an autographed picture, which I received.

The military offers an endless array of autograph possibilities. You can even write to the various military ships and airplanes and receive pictures of them, often signed by the Commanding Officer.

600 North Westshore Boulevard
Suite 1202
Tampa, Florida 33609

May 14, 1992

Dear John,

Thank you for your letter and the invitation to join you and your family for the 4th of July parade and party at Bear Run. I appreciate the invitation; however, I will be in Alaska salmon fishing with my son Christian on that day. Nevertheless, I am most appreciative of your thoughtful invitation and wish you the very best in your future endeavors.

Sincerely,

H. Norman Schwarzkopf
General, U.S. Army, Retired

Mr. John Schlimm
479 Brussels Street
St. Marys, Pennsylvania 15857

ALMA J. POWELL

Dear Mr. Schlimm,
Thank you for your very kind letter.
Alas, I have no photos to send but hope this note will suffice
Best Wishes
Alma J. Powell

Top: A letter from General H. Norman Schwarzkopf
Bottom: A note from Alma Powell

CHAPTER 7
MISCELLANEOUS POLITICAL FIGURES

Some political figures do not fit into any of the categories I have discussed so far. These include party leaders and Presidents and Chairpersons of various political organizations. For example, you can write to the Democratic and Republican Party Chairpersons and receive a signed photo.

I will also group the Directors of the Central Intelligence Agency (CIA) and Federal Bureau of Investigation (FBI) in this category. I wrote to both Directors and although I did not receive any autographs, the CIA sent a very informative booklet about the CIA and a portrait Director Woolsey.

Some of the men and women who head political organizations have had amazing careers in politics and are worth writing to for an autograph. Two of these people to whom I have written are former Ambassador Jeanne Kirkpatrick and former Congressman Vin Weber, who are both involved with Empower America.

I also wrote to former Surgeon General C. Everett Koop, who replied with an autographed portrait. Surgeon General Joycelyn Elders sent an unsigned portrait.

Astronauts are great subjects and a wonderful genre for autograph collectors. Although most of these men and women are not politicians, they are American treasures and their work is completed on behalf of the United States Government. You can write to astronauts at the various space institutions around the country or wherever else they may work. I wrote to astronaut Sally Ride and she replied with a signed portrait. John Glenn, U.S. Senator and the first astronaut to circle the earth, also sent a signed photograph. Other astronauts to whom you may want to write are Alan B. Shepard, Jr., Neil A. Armstrong, and Edwin E. Aldrin, Jr.

Washington is full of current and former political officials to whom you can write for autographs. Almost anyone with any notoriety in Washington has portraits of themselves to send to fans or autograph collectors. You have to decide for yourself to which of these officials you want to write.

To John –
John Glenn

Senator and Astronaut, John Glenn of Ohio

July 10, 1995

Mr. John E. Schlimm, II
479 Brussells Street
St. Marys, PA 15857

Dear Mr. Schlimm,

Thank you very much for your very kind note. It's always
gratifying to hear that I have been an inspiration to someone.
Congratulations on graduating Summa Cum Laude. That's quite an
accomplishment. As you requested, I have personalized your copy
of our book and return it with this note. Thanks also for being
so thoughtful as to include a return, postage-paid envelope. I
wish you and yours peace and happiness.

Sincerely,

Terry Anderson

Top: Former hostage, Terry Anderson
Bottom: C. Everett Koop

CHAPTER 8
INTERNATIONAL FIGURES

Foreign Dignitaries

One of the most difficult genres of autograph collecting to take up is writing to foreign dignitaries. However, it can be one of the most rewarding categories. There are a few things you should know and be aware of when writing to dignitaries and officials of other countries.

You can call the Embassies in Washington to get information about how to write to a particular dignitary. The State Department can also be very helpful when writing to leaders of foreign countries by supplying you with addresses and appropriate titles for world leaders. Foreign dignitaries include Presidents, First Ladies, Vice Presidents and spouses, Royals, Prime Ministers and spouses, Ambassadors and spouses, etc... The title of a dignitary in a country depends on the particular leader to whom you are writing a letter.

When writing to foreign dignitaries, you have to be very careful how you address them by name. For example, the following is how various dignitaries can be addressed in a letter: His/Her Excellency, The Right Honorable, His/Her Majesty, His/Her Royal Highness, His/Her Eminence, His Imperial Majesty, and His/Her Serene Highness.

It is important to properly address foreign dignitaries out of respect for their position and to write polite letters. Be sure to specify on your return address that you are from the U.S.A. This will be important if the official responds to your request.

It can be difficult to know how much postage to put on a letter being sent overseas. Therefore, it is wise to take your letter to the post office and let them figure out how much the postage costs. This will save you money and save you from the trouble of having your letter returned unopened. However, because other countries have different postal systems, it might be difficult to send a S.A.S.E. It would be wise to consult your local post office officials with this matter.

Since mail travel between countries varies from plane to boat and, therefore, can be fast or slow, you must be patient when waiting for a response.

One of my favorite replies from a foreign dignitary is a personally autographed picture I received from Norma Majors, wife of Prime Minister John Majors. She is the equivalent of our First Lady.

Another favorite autograph of mine from an American dignitary is a signed notecard I received from Ambassador Shirley Temple Black, former child star.

Since some foreign dignitaries may be reluctant to respond to autograph requests, you may want to send something for them to sign, such as a book they have written. I sent Raisa Gorbachev, former First Lady of the former Soviet Union, a copy of her book, I Hope, to sign. I recently received the book back, personally autographed in Russian.

Royalty

It can be very exciting to write to royalty. The most prominent royal family is the British royal family. However, there are royals all over the world, including kings, queens, princes, princesses, dukes, duchesses, lords, ladies, barons, and baronesses, etc... I have written to the British royal family and the royal family in Monaco, which are two of the most visible royal families in the world.

The only authentic signature I received was from Princess Stephanie of Monaco. I did receive photos from Prince Albert of Monaco and Prince Edward of Great Britain. The other members of the royal families did not send pictures, but rather had letters sent on their behalf explaining that because of the volume of similar requests they only sign portraits for other dignitaries and friends.

I often wonder what would happen if you met a member of the royal family, any royal family, and asked them for their autograph. I have never seen a royal giving an autograph to a commoner. I have never had the opportunity to meet a royal, but when I do, you can bet I will ask for their signature.

To John E. Schlimm II
Best Wishes,
Shirley Temple Black
1994

Top: Dr. Helmut Kohl of Germany
Bottom: Former Ambassador and child star, Shirley Temple Black

Stephanie

Daniel

CLARENCE HOUSE
S.W.1

28th January, 1994

Dear Mr. Schlimm,

Queen Elizabeth The Queen Mother has
asked me to thank you for your letter.

Her Majesty regrets that it is not
possible to grant your wish.   The reason is
that members of the Royal Family receive so many
requests for photographs and autographs that a
strict rule has had to be made that these are
only given to personal friends or for official
purposes.

I am sorry to send you this reply, which
may cause disappointment.

Yours sincerely,

Frances Campbell Preston

Lady-in-Waiting

Mr. J. E. Schlimm, II.

Top: Princess Stephanie of Monaco
Bottom: A letter from the Queen Mother's Lady-in-Waiting

Part 2

I have admired Bette Midler since the first time I saw <u>Beaches</u>.

MASS MEDIA AUTOGRAPHS

The Mass Media encompasses a global network of outlets including television, radio, movies, newspapers, and magazines. These outlets offer an endless number of stars and notable figures to which an ambitious autograph seeker can write. This large genre can be divided into several smaller genres, each equally exciting and challenging.

The most popular media stars of the moment are the most difficult, if not impossible, people from whom to receive a reply. These celebrities often receive thousands of letters from fans and at different addresses. I have found with most of these stars, my letters were never answered. It is best to wait a few years until the star is not as famous and then write them. A lot of these stars will use the Autopen or stamps for their pictures or send information about joining a fan club. You should be cautious about these replies.

Since celebrities often have several addresses to which you can send mail, try to find the most direct address. This is usually the address of the agency who handles the star. It is even better if you can find a name of someone in a celebrity's office, such as an agent, to whose attention the letter can be sent. Celebrities have huge staffs who handle their mail. If possible, include a S.A.S.E., which may encourage the star's staff to send you a reply. It is also a very good idea to put your return address on the envelope in case you have the wrong address for the celebrity. Stars are constantly moving and changing agencies and their mail is not always forwarded.

You may want to further ensure a response by sending the star something to sign, which might include magazine covers, books about or written by the star, movie posters, or any other memorabilia you might have concerning the celebrity. Also, be sure to compliment a star on their latest project, whether it is a book, television show, movie, etc...

You can also ask stars for copies of their biographies, which will be a nice addition to your collection. Be aware that a lot of people in close proximity to these stars become celebrities themselves, including family members or close associates. These people are also worth pursuing for an autograph.

Some celebrities take months to respond and others will reply within a few weeks. Response times depend on a star's work schedule and the volume of mail they receive. However, some stars, such as Katherine Hepburn, refuse to sign anything, period.

If you ever get the chance to meet a celebrity or be near one, pull out your camera and be sure to ask for a picture and an autograph. Just remember, they are not likely to ever see you again, so do not worry about looking foolish!

are not likely to ever see you again, so do not worry about looking foolish!

I have not had as much personal experience with meeting media stars as I have had with meeting politicians, but I do have a few stories that I will share with you. One of my favorite stories happened during my freshman year in college when I was volunteering at the "Best of Washington" Fashion Show, which is a charity show in which celebrities model clothes. Before the show, I was standing by the runway when this man came up to me and asked for someone. I did not know the person for whom he was asking and he went on his way. Later during the show, I recognized the same man walking down the runway. It was Larry King!

Larry King

CHAPTER 9
STARS

Television Stars

There are several celebrity address books you can buy. If you ask at your local bookstore, they will find you one. Be sure to get the most up-to-date edition available. For television stars, you can write to their studio, station, or agency.

As an experiment, I wrote to the entire cast of <u>Beverly Hills 90210</u>. Since the show was so popular at the time and I had heard that the stars got tons of mail, I was curious to see what kind of responses I would get. After several weeks, I received general newsletter-type brochures from several of the main stars, such as Luke Perry and Shannen Doherty. Some of the actors did not send anything. The one authentically autographed cast picture I received was from Carol Potter, who plays the mother on the show. I came to the conclusion that perhaps she gets the least mail out of the entire cast.

My favorite television autographs include a handwritten note from Carol Burnett, signed pictures from both Bob and Dolores Hope, a signed letter, photo, and notecard from Mr. Fred Rogers, and a personally autographed picture from Ellen Corby, who played Grandma Walton. Many older stars from years past are alive and will send out autographs upon request. Unfortunately, it is very hard to get most of these former stars' addresses.

Some television stars will send information about joining their fan clubs instead of sending autographs. It is really up to you if you want to pursue this any further.

Jacques Cousteau sent information about the Cousteau Society and made it clear in an actual fact sheet on autographs that he only signs for members of his Society and they could not find my name in their files. I am still not a member!

Celebrities often make special appearances at malls and other places on behalf of their favorite charities or while promoting a new product. Watch for advertisements about these events and go to them. The celebrities will often sign autographs at such events.

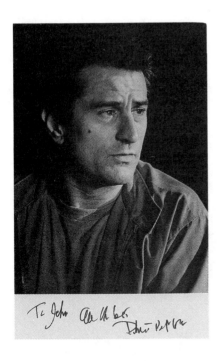

Top Left: Robert DeNiro
Top Right: Priscilla Presley
Bottom Left: Clint Eastwood
Bottom Right: Sally Field

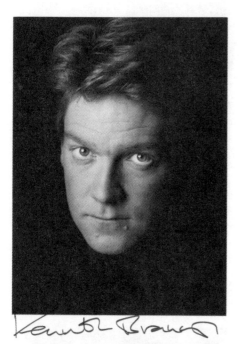

Top Left: Kenneth Branagh
Photograph by Trevor Leighton
Top Right: Kathy Bates
Bottom Left: Bob Hope
Bottom Right: Betty White

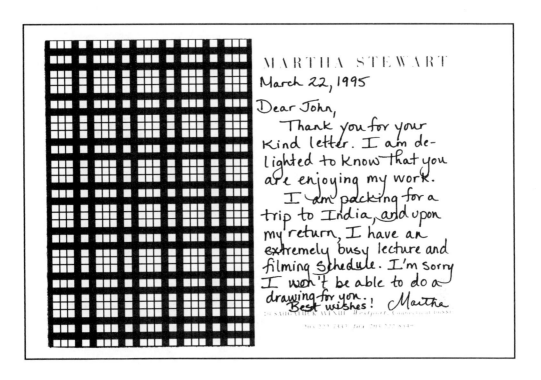

Angela Bassett

Top: A note from Martha Stewart, who fits into several genres
Bottom: A note from Angela Bassett

CAROL BURNETT

July 24, 1992

Dear John –
I hope This sample of
my hand writing is sufficient
and that your analysis
is positive!

Sincerely,
Carol Burnett

A note from Carol Burnett

Movie Stars

There is a presence about movie stars that certainly puts them in a category all to themselves. When we see them up on the big screen, they are larger than life. When you see a star in real life, they exhibit an almost transcendent aura around them. They seem somehow different than we are, even though they are just as human as we. I have had the pleasure of seeing a few movie stars in person, including Arnold Schwarzenegger and Dolph Lundgren, both of whom I saw at The 1990 Best Buddies Ball in Washington.

I would guess that movie stars make up the most popular genre in autograph collecting. No matter where a star is, there always seems to be someone asking for their autograph. Besides requests in person, millions of fans write to their favorite movie stars every year asking for autographs and other items. I have written to a few current and older movie stars. I have received a few autographed portraits, but not nearly as many replies as the requests I sent out.

Some of my favorite signed pictures of movie stars are from Jimmy Stewart, Sophia Loren, Whoopi Goldberg, Steven Seagal, Shirley McLain, Jane Fonda, Michael Caine, Dudley Moore, and Sigourney Weaver. It can be extremely exciting when a celebrity sends a promotional picture from one of their movies. Sigourney Weaver sent a signed picture of her character from Aliens III. I also acquired a signed movie poster from Jean-Claude Van Damme.

There are a few things to keep in mind when writing to movie stars. First, realize that you are one in millions of fans who are writing to any one famous star. It might be more rewarding to write to some of the older celebrities who may not get as much mail as their younger counterparts. Second, be sure to get the right address for the star. Just like TV stars, movie stars may have several addresses, including those for their homes, studios, fan clubs, and agents. There are several books on the market with addresses of stars. Be sure to get a reliable and the most up-to-date address book you can. Who's Who In America is always a very reliable source for addresses. Third, because of the volume of mail a star receives, a response could take several months. Fourth, to help ensure a response, you may want to send an item, such as a book, for the celebrity to sign. Finally, it is always a good idea to send a S.A.S.E.

Unfortunately, as with many politicians, you can never be completely sure that the actual celebrity signed their own signature. The value of your collection will be based on those autographs you can verify as real. However, the most important part of collecting signatures is to have fun.

People associated with movie stars are worthy subjects for autograph seekers. It is thrilling to write to spouses and children of movie stars, because most of them are usually mini celebrities because of their relationship with the movie star.

Newscasters

In the last decade or so, the people who bring the news into our homes every day have become quite famous celebrities. As a country, we have become interested in the lives of famous newscasters, such as Connie Chung, Katie Couric, Bryant Gumble, Dan Rathers, Jane Pauley, Sam Donaldson, Peter Jennings, Barbara Walters, and any number of CNN personalities, to name a few. Through the work I did at The White House, I was afforded several opportunities to meet and speak with some of these famous news personalities.

Mrs. Gore's Press Secretary, Sally Aman, with whom I directly worked included me in as much as possible and I owe her a great debt of gratitude for allowing me to meet a lot of these people. One day, I got to escort Connie Chung up to Mrs. Gore's Office and sit in on the interview. As I was escorting Connie Chung out of the building, I asked her to sign a copy of Ladies' Home Journal since she was on the cover. She wrote: "It was great to meet you....I'll let you know when my next interview is and you can sit in." She was such a charming and beautiful woman. It was funny to first see her sitting in the lobby of the Old Executive Office Building alone. Here was this famous woman that we see every night and no one seemed to notice her. I suspect she likes the anonymity every once in a while.

On another occasion, I escorted CNN's Judy Woodruff to Mrs. Gore's Office. At first, I was intimidated by this serious looking woman with very defined features. I have to admit, I did not even know what she looked like before she came that day. As I watched her and her style, I became one of her biggest fans. As I escorted her out of the Old Executive Office Building, I asked her to sign a piece of the Vice President's stationery.

My final experience in this genre was with Katie Couric. I went with Sally and Mrs. Gore one day for a taping of the Today Show. As I sat in the Green Room, which is the name for the room all shows use to hold guests and their staffs, I connected eyes with this woman who was racing by outside the door. I simply smiled and then she came in and introduced herself: "Hi, I'm Katie Couric!" I did not even recognize her at first and I was caught somewhat off guard. I had written to her months before for an autographed portrait which I received, so I did not feel it was appropriate to ask for her signature on this

Top: Barbara Walters
Bottom: Katie Couric

*To John
Thanks*

You and your children are cordially invited to attend a Halloween Party

Saturday, October 30, 1993
two to four o'clock
at The Vice President's House
34th Street and Massachusetts Avenue, Northwest
Washington, DC
R.s.v.p. 202-456-7077

**Jay Leno signed this for me at Vice President Gore's Halloween party
Along with his autograph, Jay Leno also draws a caricature of himself**

occasion. I did love the experience of sitting in on the live interview. The stage that Katie and Mrs. Gore sat on was so small. It looks so much larger on television!

When writing to these news figures, it is best to send letters to the studios where their various shows are taped or to the network on which they appear. This is convenient, because several of these people can be written to at the same address. When writing, keep in mind that these newscasters get large amounts of mail on numerous issues, so be patient when waiting for a reply.

Some of my favorite autographs in this genre are from Connie Chung, Judy Woodruff, Katie Couric, Barbara Walters, Diane Sawyer, Hugh Downs, Dan Rather, Sam Donaldson, and Catherine Crier.

It can be in your best interest to also write to the less notable newscasters, including reporters from your local stations. You never know who the stars of tomorrow are going to be!

Talk Show Hosts

Just like newscasters, talk show hosts come into our homes everyday and have become interesting to us as celebrity personalities. I have successfully written to several of these dynamic people for autographed photos, including Oprah Winfrey, Jay Leno, David Letterman (my favorite), Joan Rivers, and Rush Limbaugh.

I had the distinct pleasure of meeting two of these great performers. I was helping with the 1993 Halloween press party at The Vice President's Residence, when I found myself talking to Jay Leno. As I was standing by the back door, Jay Leno and his wife walked down the hall to leave, but we could not find his umbrella. After sending another volunteer in search of the umbrella, I spoke with Mr. Leno. He asked me what my major was and when I told him, he replied, "So, you're doing that Communications thing!" He really is a very funny and polite man. I could not believe I was standing in Al Gore's house talking with Jay Leno! I asked him to sign my party invitation. Along with his signature, he also draws a caricature of himself. He also did this on his portrait I had received months before.

I also got to meet Joan Rivers at a horse race in Virginia. No one even recognized her at first. My friend and I followed her back to her car where I finally got up the nerve to talk to her. She was so gracious and even joked about her dog, who had been attacked by a larger dog a few minutes earlier. I later wrote to her explaining how I enjoyed meeting her and she sent me a beautiful, signed picture of herself holding her Emmy award.

These special stars make up a most unique genre for autograph seekers. Talk show hosts can be written to at their studios or agencies. As you can imagine, they also receive a huge amount of mail and you should not expect a quick response. It took several months for me to get a signed picture of David Letterman. It was worth the wait!

Game Show Hosts

You can write to your favorite game show hosts. Some of these men and women have become very famous, such as Bob Barker, Alex Trebek, and Vanna White. If you are interested in this genre, it can be very rewarding. Mail your requests to the studio where the game show is taped or to the agent who handles the particular game show personality.

When I wrote to Alex Trebek asking for a sample of his handwriting for my graphology project, he wrote back: "When you analyze my handwriting, be kind."

Singers

From Rock 'N' Roll to Polka, singing stars can claim as many fans and followers as television and movie stars. Rock stars, such as Madonna and Michael Jackson, are even more famous than many leading stars of the big screen and even more popular for autograph seekers. Since many of these men and women are off touring around the world, it can take a long time for them to reply and it sometimes is even harder to get their addresses in the first place. It is wise to consult the various address books available for the names of these stars' agencies and offices. Sometimes, singing stars' addresses will be the recording companies they are signed under. Be careful to whom you write, because the more popular a singing star is, the least likely you are to receive an authentically signed photo. However, this is not always true.

Some of my favorite, personalized autographs of singing stars are from Elton John, Barbara Mandrell, Kenny Rogers, and Cher. As you can see from my eclectic collection, you can take this huge genre and break it down into several genres based on the type of music singers perform. A few smaller genres are Rock, Country, Jazz, Opera, Instrumental, and Progressive.

My most embarrassing autograph request so far was when I wrote to the

Top Left: Reba McEntire
Top Right: Naomi Judd
Bottom Left: Dolly Parton
Bottom Right: Cher

Top Left: Orville Redenbacher
Top Right: Vanna White
Bottom: Dave Thomas

world famous Conductor Leonard Bernstein. I was not aware that he had died, but only wrote because I knew the name was famous. I received a polite letter from his agency. They must have thought I was a real fool. I sure felt like one!

Famous Animals

The purpose of this section is to make you aware that you can write to your favorite, famous animals just as you can write to your favorite Presidential Pets. Over the years, two of the more famous animals have been Lassie and Morris the Cat.

As ridiculous as it may seem, address your letter to the particular animal and send the letter to the animal's studio or agent. Yes, even animals have agents! It will be great fun and, if nothing else, an interesting experiment to see what you are sent back.

Commercial Stars

Many of the actors who appear in commercials have become big time stars. My favorite autograph from this genre is a handwritten note I received from Frank Perdue, who owns Perdue Farms Incorporated and who appears in commercials promoting his chicken. He wrote: "It's nice to hear from you and I'm happy to respond to such a well-mannered and talented young man." I also like the signed picture I received from Orville Redenbacher, who sent a picture of himself enjoying his favorite snack. Sausage king Jimmy Dean and "Wendy's" favorite dad, Dave Thomas, also sent me signed pictures.

In these cases, I was able to write directly to the four men's companies for their autographs. It is more difficult to get the addresses of the actors who perform in commercials. You can try writing to the headquarters of the company whose product the actors are promoting. You should watch for any public appearances these actors might be making and be sure to go to the event.

Producers and Directors

Many producers and directors have become as famous as the stars they finance and direct. Four of the most famous figures in this genre are Steven Speilberg, Oliver Stone, Kathleen Kennedy, and Aaron Spelling. Many of these men and women run their own companies named after them. The most direct way to reach these people is to write to their production companies or offices. It will make your collection even more interesting if you send these producers and directors an item related to one of their projects to sign.

Sometimes, directors and actors switch roles. When I wrote to Spike Lee for an autograph, he sent me a signed picture of his character Shorty from Malcolm X.

My most prized autograph in this genre is from Aaron Spelling. I wrote to him for a sample of his handwriting and he replied with a wonderful, handwritten note, which reads in part: "Good Luck in college. I only wish my handwriting could match yours."

A note from Aaron Spelling

Part 3

To John —

Best wishes from your

#1 fan *Stephen King*

5/31/94

One of my favorite book inscriptions from Stephen King

WRITERS' AUTOGRAPHS

     Writers make up a very special genre for autograph collectors. The men and women who write books and news columns are among the most accessible subjects for autograph seekers. I started writing for signed books about two years ago and I have since built up a collection of over one hundred, personally signed books. I also started writing to the people who report the news in newspapers and magazines.

COSMOPOLITAN

Helen Gurley Brown

Dear John

Here a sample of my hand writing "...

it's pretty Bad !

Helen Gurley Brown

THE HEARST CORPORATION

A note from Helen Gurley Brown

CHAPTER 10
AUTOGRAPHED BOOKS

I have found that many people who will not respond to a general request for an autograph seem more than willing to sign a copy of a book they have written.   In fact, sending books is often the only way you will get some autographs, especially signatures of former Presidents. I wrote to Richard Nixon several times for an autographed picture and never received one. Finally, I bought one of his books for $1.00. I mailed the book to him and a few weeks later it came back personally signed. It is even more special to me than many of my other books because a few months later President Nixon passed away.

You can often find books in bargain piles at bookstores for under $5.00. I often go to stores not knowing whose book I may find for a cheap price to send out. I paid $1.00 for Ronald Reagan's memoirs and now it, too, is autographed. I do pay full price sometimes for books I want to read and then I send those books to the authors to sign. Books are of no use just lying around the house. You can send paperbacks, but I advise only sending hardbacks. Hardbacks are made stronger than paperbacks and will last longer.

The best way to send a book is to put it in a padded mailing envelope along with your letter and a S.A.S.E. In no other genre is a S.A.S.E. as important as it is when sending books. You must have a S.A.S.E. or the author probably will not be able to return your book because of the expense. It is also best to seal your envelope by stapling or taping it shut to ensure it will not open along the way.

One term that you should familiarize yourself with when mailing books is "Book Rate". The Book Rate is a special rate of postage the post office offers when you are mailing books. You should write "Book Rate" on both of your envelopes and take them to the post office where they will be weighed and properly stamped. This will save you money. When I originally started mailing books, I guessed at the postage. When I started taking the packages to the post office for the Book Rate, I was so surprised at how much money I saved on stamps.

This genre of autograph collecting has quickly become one of my favorites. I have sent books to a wide array of celebrities for them to sign. Some of the authors I have written include: John Grisham, Michael Crichton, Stephen King, Barbara Bush, Nancy Reagan, Marilyn Quayle, Kitty Kelley, Sonny Bono, George Burns, Dan Rather, Sam Donaldson, Jimmy Carter, Bob Hope, Jimmy Stewart, Bob Woodward, and Roseanne. Other autographed books I have received either in person or through contacts include books by Tipper Gore, Al

Gore, Dan Quayle, Oliver North, and Margaret Thatcher.

As with any autographs, it can be very exciting to have an author sign his book in person for you. You should watch at your local bookstores for book signings, which authors attend to promote their new books. It is amazing how many people attend these events. You should check with a bookstore prior to a book signing and find out how early you should get there to make sure you will get a signed book. Sometimes a celebrity is on a tight schedule and the line has to be cut. If you do not make it to a book signing, contact the bookstore to see if they have extra copies of the signed book. I was able to get signed copies of Naomi Judd's <u>Love Can Build A Bridge</u> and Mary Matalin and James Carville's <u>All's Fair</u> because the store had extra copies after the signing.

The very first book signing I attended was for Maya Angelou's book, <u>Wouldn't Take Nothing For My Journey Now</u>. I actually wanted her to sign my copy of the Inaugural Poem, <u>On The Pulse Of Morning</u>, which she wrote. After waiting almost two hours, the line was cut about twenty people in front of me. I later learned that if I would have waited, she probably would have signed the book.

Several months later, Maya Angelou was a special guest at an event at The Vice President's Residence. I went armed with another copy of the Inaugural poem (I had sent the first copy to her to sign, but had not yet received it) and a copy of her new book. When I finally introduced myself to Ms. Angelou and asked her to sign the books, she said she could not autograph them because it would have created an autographing clutch around her. I felt like I was not meant to have her books signed.

After I came home that summer, I decided to give it one more try. By looking on the book sleeve, I had found out that Ms. Angelou is a Reynolds Professor at Wake Forest University in North Carolina. I sent the books to the university and explained how I had met her at the Gores' house. A few weeks later, I not only got back the two books I sent, but I also received the original copy of the poem I had sent several months before and they were all personally autographed. On top of that, she sent a personally handwritten note. I was thrilled beyond words and am now one of her greatest admirers!

The second book signing I attended was for Dan Quayle's memoirs. I am happy to write that I made it to the front this time and he signed two copies of his book for me.

Two very interesting things have happened since I have been sending out books to authors. First, the only person to send a book back unsigned is Frank Sinatra. Second, after sending three books to Stephen King, I received a note from his assistant saying that Mr. King has a policy of only signing two books per customer. Since he had already signed three for me, Mr. King's assistant basically said I am not allowed to send anymore books. My opinion on this is if you are a fan of an author and willing to buy their books, they could at least be willing to sign the books for you!

Just to be fair to Stephen King, I have to admit that he wrote one of the best inscriptions to me out of all the other authors. In my copy of <u>Misery</u>, Mr. King wrote: "To John....Best Wishes From Your #1 Fan....Stephen King."

The most endearing and my most treasured book inscription is from Mrs. Gore, who wrote: "To John....I cannot thank you enough for all of your help this year. You are the best. I don't know how we're going to cope without you but good luck. Remember that we love you! Love, Tipper Gore."

An inscription from John Grisham

CHAPTER 11
COLUMNISTS AND REPORTERS

Many of the writers who report the news daily in newspapers and magazines have very interesting personalities and have become fun to watch and follow. A lot of these men and women appear on talk shows and have become real opinion leaders on a wide range of issues.

The White House Press Corp, which consists of the reporters who monitor the day-to-day happenings at The White House, has many colorful characters. Two of my favorite reporters from The White House are UPI reporter Helen Thomas, who has covered The White House for several decades, and Sarah McClendon of the McClendon News Service, who has also covered Washington politics for over 50 years. I wrote to both of these women. I received a wonderful note from Ms. McClendon, which reads in part: "Greetings and all good wishes from a Washington reporter who has been covering the news here for 50 years, who at age 85 is continuing to work to the fullest to improve her country and keep it alive."

Other favorites of mine include an autograph from gossip columnist Cindy Adams of The New York Post, a signed photo and notecard from satirist Art Buchwald, and two signed pictures and a notecard from Pat Buchanan, who fits into several genres including columnist, talk show host, and candidate for President of the United States.

One of the most personal and charming autographs I received was from Helen Gurley Brown, Editor at Cosmopolitan. After writing to her for a sample of her handwriting, she replied with a handwritten note saying: "Here's a sample of my handwriting....It's pretty bad!"

When writing to these reporters, you can send the letters directly to the publication at which they work. I have found that most of these people will reply with notes rather than pictures, although I have received some photos. Some of the reporters will not respond unless you send a book they have written or other items. I wrote to Bob Woodward, a reporter for The Washington Post, several times without receiving a response. I started sending him copies of his books to sign and I have received each one back personally autographed.

PATRICK J. BUCHANAN

Aug 11/92

Dear Mr. Schlinn:

Herewith, my signature.

Pat Buchanan

All the Best / PJB

To John —
with best wishes

Peter Benchley

4.17.95

Robert Waller

Top: A note from Pat Buchanan
Bottom Left: Peter Benchley, <u>Jaws</u>
Bottom Right: Robert James Waller, <u>The Bridges of Madison County</u>

To John

Caroline Kennedy

To John,
With love & Good Luck,
Happy Reading!
Jackie Collins

November
1994

Margaret Thatcher

Top Left: Caroline Kennedy
Top Right: I stood for 3 hours to get this autograph from Colin Powell
Bottom Left: Jackie Collins
Bottom Right: Margaret Thatcher

Part 4

One of my favorite artists, Roy Lichtenstein

ARTISTS' AUTOGRAPHS

There is no question about the value of an artist's work and signature. Since most of us cannot afford an original piece of art from famous artists or even a signed print, it can be very rewarding to write to an artist for an autograph. As with any autograph, a signature from a real artist is in itself an original piece of art by its creator. If we look at it this way, we can all own an original work by an artist.

This large genre can be broken into several categories based on your own personal interests in art. I have divided it into artists in general, which includes painters, drawers, sculptors, etc..., photographers, fashion designers, which I have also grouped with models since they so often go hand-in-hand, and cartoonists and their characters. There are numerous other categories of artists to which you can write including architects and interior designers, but I have limited my writing to these few categories that I think are of the most interest to the most people and most interesting to me. However, you should focus on the category that most interests you and write to those artists.

You can write to artists at their studios, galleries, companies, and agencies. There are several books with addresses of various artists, including <u>Who's Who in American Art</u>. Be sure to get an updated address. You should be aware, as with many other celebrities, there are some artists who will not send out their autograph.

Annie Leibovitz

CHAPTER 12
ARTISTS OF THE WORLD

Artists

Three of the major artists to whom I have written are Christo, Roy Lichtenstein, and George Segal. Each of these men have responded to my requests in very different and unique ways: Christo sent me several signed postcards of his work, which thrilled me because they are like small, signed prints; Mr. Lichtenstein sent a signed notecard with a most interesting stamp at the top; and Mr. Segal sent a postcard of one of his sculptures and wrote a note on the back of it.

If you are interested in art, this genre will be very fascinating to you. There are several possibilities when writing to artists. You could send them a print of their work and see if they will sign it. If you do this, put the print in a mailing tube and take it to the post office to have the correct postage put on it. Since it might be difficult to include a S.A.S.E., you might want to put the stamps in the tube, so that the artist can re-use the tube when mailing the print back to you.

Another possibility is to mail an artist a book of his work to sign. Of course, you can always send a notecard or ask for a portrait of the artist. You could also send a blank canvas or piece of paper and ask the artist to sketch or doodle something for you. You might be surprised at what you get back. I sent Mr. Rogers a blank canvas and he replied by drawing music notes on it. Even though he is not an actual artist, I now have a picture drawn by Fred Rogers!

Photographers

There are several famous photographers in the world. Photographers are among the most talented artists because they have to combine every element of what makes art work into their pictures. This is a particular favorite genre of mine, because I am an amateur photographer and so I can appreciate what these great men and women do for a living.

The one photographer I have written to is Annie Leibovitz, who has taken portraits of celebrities for several years and whose work can be seen in several books and magazines. She replied by sending me the most creative portrait I have received to date. It is a signed black and white picture of her running, camera in hand, across the roof of a building with the New York skyline in the background.

More and more, celebrities from other fields, such as movie stars and politicians, are becoming photographers. My favorite photographer from this category is Tipper Gore. She has been an avid photographer since her husband gave her a camera in 1974. As the Second Lady, she carries her camera with her almost everywhere and captures history in the making. Her photographs have been published in magazines and displayed in exhibits, including her very own exhibit of photographs from the Presidential campaign called "Campaign 1992 Close-up". I am thrilled to write that I have a signed photograph Mrs. Gore took of The Vice President's Residence to commemorate its 100th Anniversary in 1993.

Fashion Designers and Models

Few people realize or even think about fashion designers as artists, but they are some of the finest and most talented artists in the world. Fabric is their medium and they create sculptures for the body. I have written to numerous designers and asked for signed pictures.

I have found that fashion designers send out some of the most creative portraits of any genre. This is a direct reflection of their artistic tastes and talents. Some of my favorite signed portraits are of Calvin Klein, Geoffrey Beene, Giorgio Armani, Diane Von Furstenburg, and Bill Blass. I have written to both Liz Claiborne and Estee Lauder only to find that the former retired in 1989 and dedicates herself to the Liz Claiborne and Art Ortenberg Foundation and the latter does not sign photographs for public distribution. However, Estee Lauder did send me a free sample of the Lauder for Men fragrance. There are many benefits to writing for autographs!

One of the friendliest designers is Donna Karan. I have written to her twice requesting information about her clothes and her company and each time I have received a thick packet of photographs and information. The first time I wrote to Ms. Karan, I included three of her ads from a magazine to see if she would sign them. They all came back signed in gold!

I got a signed portrait of designer Bob Mackie when I met him at Tyson's Corner in Virginia. He was at the mall to promote his newest fragrance. Mr. Mackie is well known for the outrageous and glamorous clothes he has designed for such stars as Cher.

I have grouped models into this category although they could be a genre all to themselves. It is possible to write to famous models through their agencies and agents. I was fortunate to meet Supermodel Cindy Crawford at The White House while she was taping a segment for MTV. She autographed a piece of the Vice President's stationery for me. I have never seen such a perfect human being!

Cartoonists and Characters

The work that goes into drawing cartoons and bringing them to life is fantastic. The men and women who bring us these wonderful characters are multi-talented for they can draw pictures that tell us a story, which might make us laugh, cry, or even incite anger. Two of my favorite cartoonists are Matt Groening, who among other things gave birth to Bart Simpson, and Gary Trudeau, whose political cartoon "Doonesbury" has drawn both criticism and praise.

Both of these men replied to my requests in most unique ways: Mr. Groening sent me a picture of the Simpsons on which he actually drew a sketch of Bart's head and wrote a nice message and Mr. Trudeau sent a piece of "Doonesbury" stationery personally signed and filled with "Doonesbury" stamps and stickers.

These fine men and women can be reached at the publications for which they work or through their offices. It would be fun to send a cartoonist a strip of his work or even a book of his cartoons for him to sign.

Drawing by Fred Rogers

OFFICE OF THE VICE PRESIDENT

WASHINGTON, DC

I got this signature from Cindy Crawford at The White House

Schlimm II - 58

Part 5

Michael Jordan

CHAPTER 13
SPORTS AUTOGRAPHS

Athletes are among the most admired and most respected figures in the world. Sports personalities are similar to politicians in that they are seemingly average people who have risen through the ranks to reach the top. This ladder of success can be documented by collecting trading cards, which are available for almost every sporting activity. For this same reason, as in politics, it is wise to watch college athletes who show great promise and get their autographs early on when they are the most accessible. You should focus on the genre of sports that most interests you and write to those athletes.

There are several opportunities to get an athlete's autograph, including card shows, special appearances, written requests, or meeting the players before or after games. My friends and I enjoy going to watch our "home" team, the Pittsburgh Pirates. My favorite part of the game is going down to the field before the start and trying to get an autograph or waiting by the players' cars after the game and trying to get a signature.

I was amazed at how many fans wait by a player's car with baseballs, cards, T-shirts, pictures, and magazines to be signed. I had a variety of items signed, such as a magazine autographed by Andy Van Slyke and a baseball card signed by my favorite player, Jay Bell. It really is fun running from car to car and player to player trying to get as many signatures as possible. The luckiest little kids have each parent running to a different player for them while they and perhaps a sibling or friend chase other players. Some of those youngsters walk away with a lot of autographs! I am always jealous!

You can send trading cards and other items to players and coaches for them to sign. It is not very hard to find an address for a particular team. A good place to look for a team's address is in the team magazine, which you can purchase at the stadium. When sending for an autograph, whether or not you have enclosed an item to be signed, you must enclose a S.A.S.E. if you want a response.

Once during a Pirates/Braves game weekend, my friends and I stayed at the same hotel as the Braves players. Many fans waited in the lobby for the players to come down from their rooms. I did manage to ask David Justice to sign my baseball card, but he refused and brushed me away. Most of the other players were very gracious and willing to accommodate their young fans.

It is also fun to write to team mascots. I wrote to the Pirate Parrot for an autograph and I received a personally signed portrait of the famous bird and a hand-drawn sketch of the Parrot on the envelope.

Since I am not a huge sports fan, my autograph collection in this category is not too large. I do have a basketball signed by Wilt Chamberlain, which I was lucky to catch at The 1990 Best Buddies Ball. One of my prized autographs is a signed picture of Nancy Kerrigan, which I received a week before she competed in the 1994 Winter Olympic Games in Norway. I did not even have her complete address, but I knew she lived in Stoneham, Massachusetts, and so I simply addressed the letter to "Nancy Kerrigan....Stoneham, Massachusetts". When I later wrote after the Olympics, I received a photo with a facsimile of her signature. I did write to Tonya Harding, but have never heard back.

During my time at The White House, I was able to get a few sports figures' autographs in person. My most memorable sports autograph is from a member of the Washington Bullets basketball team. I met him at The 1994 White House Easter Egg Role. I had taken a picture of The White House for celebrities to sign. As I was walking on the South Lawn I saw a clutch of autograph seekers around this extremely tall man. From his uniform, I realized he played for the Bullets, but I did not know who he was. As I stood waiting my turn, a woman came up to me and asked who the guy was. I said I did not know and that I just wanted an autograph. What I did not realize was his assistant was standing next to me. The assistant, with great sarcasm, said to me, "You DON'T know who this is?" Embarrassingly, I replied I was just joking. I quickly got the signature and ran!

Bonnie Blair

Greg Louganis
Olympic Gold Medalist

SPEEDO

Nancy Kerrigan

ProServ
1101 Wilson Boulevard
Arlington, VA 22209
(703) 276-3030

Top Left: Greg Louganis
Top Right: Nancy Kerrigan
Bottom: Magic Johnson

Schlimm II - 62

Part 6

A facsimile of Pope John Paul II's signature

CHAPTER 14
RELIGIOUS AUTOGRAPHS

There are several religious figures who have become celebrities in their own right. The most famous, modern religious personalities are the Pope, Mother Teresa of Calcutta, Ralph Reed, and televangelists, such as Billy Graham and Pat Robertson.

I wrote to Pope John Paul II, but since the Pope receives so much mail it is forwarded to various church officials who are directed to answer the letters on the Pope's behalf. The reply I received was sent by Monsignor L. Sandri. He sent a small portrait of the Pope with a facsimile signature.

My most cherished religious autograph is from Mother Teresa. I wrote to her in India at her Missionaries of Charity Organization. She replied with a signed note, which reads in part: "In India, as in many other places, we have many poor children in our homes, who have no parents. That is why you must thank God for giving you wonderful parents who love you very much." Mother Teresa has been christened Saint of the Gutters, so I have no doubt she will be canonized a heavenly saint someday. I am so thrilled to have this special relic.

I also have a signed portrait of televangelist Pat Robertson, who ran for President of the United States in 1988.

You can get addresses for these religious figures from a variety of sources, including address books and by asking officials at your local church. If you are particularly interested in this genre of autographs, you can write to an endless number of bishops, cardinals, priests, televangelists, etc... Be sure to include a S.A.S.E. with your requests.

+LDM

MISSIONARIES OF CHARITY
54/A, A. J. C. Bose Road,
Calcutta - 700016. India

Dear John,

In India, as in many other places, we have many poor children in our homes, who have no parents. That is why you must thank God for giving you wonderful parents who love you very much. I want you to pray together with me for all the poor children in the world, that they too like you and I, have a chance to be loved and to love. Ask your parents to teach you how to pray. For the fruit of prayer is love, and the fruit of love is sharing the joy of loving.

God bless you.

Mother Teresa

Part 7

Ted Kennedy, patriarch of one of the world's most famous families

CHAPTER 15
BUSINESS AND FAMOUS FAMILY AUTOGRAPHS

Many wealthy and powerful business people and their families have become very famous because of their extravagant lifestyles and immense riches. Some family names that immediately come to mind are the Kennedys, Rockefellers, Trumps, DuPonts, and the Disneys. These families have captivated the country and the world with successes and scandalizing headlines that have turned these people into instant celebrities.

My favorite family to write is the Kennedys. So far, I have received autographs on books, notes, or portraits from Caroline Kennedy Schlossberg, Senator Edward "Ted" Kennedy, Eunice Kennedy Shriver, Sargent Shriver (former Presidential candidate), Ethel Kennedy, Ambassador Jean Kennedy Smith, Joan Kennedy, Representative Joe Kennedy, and Anthony Kennedy Shriver. I was able to get autographs from these family members because their addresses are public knowledge. There are still a lot of Kennedys from whom I would like autographs, especially John F. Kennedy, Jr.

Some other famous family members and business tycoons who have sent me autographs include Roy Disney, Pete DuPont, Donald Trump, Malcolm Forbes, Jr., and Lee Iacocca.

These celebrity families and business figures can be written to at their homes, if you can find the addresses, or at their places of business, for which it should be easier to find addresses. Be sure to include a S.A.S.E., especially if you are sending the request to the person's home address.

To JOHN SCHLIMM —
GOOD LUCK !

Lee Iacocca.

Lee Iacocca

Part 8

Lawyer Johnnie Cochran from the O.J. Simpson trial

CHAPTER 16
CONTROVERSIAL AUTOGRAPHS

Over the past decade, the media has taken ordinary people and made them into superstars. Among these ordinary people, are criminals, victims of crime, lawyers, and just about any person who does something newsworthy. A few examples from this genre are John and Lorena Bobbitt, Rodney King, Alan Dershowitz, Robert Shapiro, Marcia Clark, Michael Milken, Susan Smith, and Charles Manson. It seems like all one has to do is commit a crime and they and everyone connected to them will become celebrities.

As controversial as it is, crime memorabilia is very popular and includes such items as comic books and trading cards depicting the crimes, weapons used by the criminal, works of art by the criminal, and autographs. I have to admit that it is a fascinating genre, if not a bit demented. Personally, I would be afraid to write to such figures as Charles Manson and his followers.

I do have a story about one criminal to whom I wrote. I found an address for Junk Bond king Michael Milken, who was sent to prison for criminal activities. I wrote to him requesting an autograph, for no other reason than that the media had made him famous. A few months later, I received a phone call from Mr. Milken's secretary who told me that somehow my letter made it to Mr. Milken in jail, who, in turn, asked her to call and let me know that he does not sign autographs. I was so stunned and impressed by this call!

If you want to write to any criminals, you can usually locate addresses for prisons, but I strongly caution you to be careful as to whom you write. You can also write to victims and lawyers of famous cases, usually by sending the letter to their home or office.

Watch in newspapers, magazines, and on the news for information about where these people live and work or where they are going to be imprisoned. It will make finding the addresses a lot easier.

Since prisoners may not have anything to send their autographs out on or since other people involved in a famous case might not have anything to sign either, it will make your project more interesting if you send something for these people to sign; perhaps something from their case: A news article, magazine cover, T-shirt, trading card, etc... Be sure to enclose a S.A.S.E.

Criminals are not the only celebrities in this genre. The victims have become just as well known. For example, it is possible to write beating victim Rodney King and ask for an autograph. And, during the Lorena Bobbitt trial in Virginia, T-shirts signed by John Wayne Bobbitt were a hot item.

Lawyers to famous criminals have also become media stars. Four of the most notable lawyers are Alan Dershowitz, Robert Shapiro, Johnnie Cochran, and F. Lee Bailey. You can write to these people at their offices for autographs. I have signed pictures of all four.

Lawyer Robert Shapiro from the O.J. Simpson trial

John Wayne Bobbitt

Schlimm II - 70

A caricature of David Letterman done by Steve Troha as part of an art class I taught at my alma mater, Elk County Christian High School. The drawing corresponds with <u>Project 12</u> in this section.

CHAPTER 17
CORRESPONDING WITH HISTORY:
PROJECTS FOR TEACHERS

There is no better way of teaching students about the world in which they live than to encourage them to interact with the people, places, and histories of their world. I believe students can learn and enjoy more of what they are learning if they are given the chance to correspond directly with the people and subjects about whom they are learning.

I have worked on several school projects where I directly wrote to the people about whom the project was based. For my "Writing for the Media" course, I was assigned to write a speech for someone whom I greatly admired. I wrote a commencement address for First Lady Barbara Bush. The speech was written to coincide with an actual graduation speech she was delivering at Marquette University in Milwaukee, Wisconsin. After I completed the speech, my professor encouraged me to send a copy to Mrs. Bush via her Executive Assistant. Several weeks later, I received a signed letter from the First Lady, which reads in part:

> What a very good Marquette commencement speech you wrote with me in mind, and how impressed I am by your talent and enterprise! The central ideas you expressed so well were also important in my remarks, and I am gratified to know that a gifted young person like you shares the values that mean so much to me....Thank you for thinking of me in such an eloquent way, and please keep writing. George Bush and I love to be reminded -- as you have reminded me -- that America's future is in very good hands.

Mrs. Bush's letter not only inspired me to continue writing, but it inspired me to write to other notable figures for autographs and other items.

The next year in my "Public Relations Techniques" course, I was assigned an independent project of my choice. I decided to create a fictional organization that Mrs. Marilyn Quayle would found. I completed a public relations plan and all of the promotional materials for the "Grand Opening". The organization I created was "C.H.A.T. With Parents"; C.H.A.T. is an acronym for Children Having A Talk With Parents. When I completed the four month project, I sent a copy to the former Second Lady in Indianapolis, Indiana. I enclosed portraits of Mrs. Quayle and her husband to be signed.   Several weeks later, both of the pictures came back signed.

The last college project on which I worked involving historical figures was my final Communications research paper. The paper was titled:

The Ladies of The White House:
An Examination of the Communications Process Between
A First and Second Lady, A Press Secretary, & The Media

I was originally inspired to write a paper about Press Secretaries because during my entire senior year of college I had the distinct honor of directly working with Mrs. Tipper Gore's Press Secretary, Sally Aman, at The White House. My time in Mrs. Gore's Office was the most educational and rewarding time of my life. Sally, who is the first Press Secretary to serve a Vice President's wife, is the best at what she does and I owe her a debt of gratitude for sharing history with me.

As part of my research, I interviewed Sally and I wrote to all of the former, living Press Secretaries to Presidents and First Ladies. From each Press Secretary, I requested a signed picture and a letter explaining what being a Press Secretary meant to them. I received responses from almost everyone to whom I had written.   The replies varied in subject and matter. I was sent letters, portraits, excerpts from books, and even a signed book. Mrs. Rosalynn Carter's former Press Secretary, Mary Finch Hoyt, sent her phone number in case I had any further questions and Mrs. Lady Bird Johnson's former Press Secretary, Liz Carpenter, sent a signed copy of her book, Ruffles & Flourishes. These letters and items are so personal and represent small snippets of history from the very people who helped to mold that history.

When I completed the paper, I gave a copy to Sally to whom I dedicated the paper. I also mailed copies to Ms. Finch and Ms. Carpenter, who both wrote back with very kind words about the paper.

I hope I have sufficiently demonstrated how beneficial and rewarding projects involving notable and historical figures can be for you and your students. During my four years of college, I not only worked on projects involving well-known personalities, but I also started an autograph collection. I first wrote to all of the Presidents and First Ladies and then I expanded my writing to other genres. Over the next few years, I amassed a collection of over one thousand autographs, including pictures, letters, books, etc...

I did not originally intend for my hobby to be a learning experience, but as I continued to receive replies I began to realize just how educational autograph collecting can be for an enthusiastic collector and, indeed, for students in a classroom. I started learning the names of U.S. Senators and House Members, State Officials, and Governors and First Ladies.

My intention in this chapter is to outline projects that you, as a teacher either at school or in the home, can incorporate into your course curriculum. I have tried to present projects for almost every school subject and grade level, but certainly each assignment can be adapted into a form that works best for you and your students. I believe that students will respond well to these projects and hopefully, in the process, they will learn more about the people and world around them.

PROJECT 1

SUBJECT:
Kindergarten and Lower Grades

ASSIGNMENT:
Have the students send a letter to their favorite cartoon character or entertainer. For example, you might encourage the students to write to Mickey and Minnie Mouse, Barney, Lamb Chop, Big Bird, Teenage Mutant Ninja Turtles, Superman, Mr. Rogers, etc...

INSTRUCTIONS:
1. As a class, discuss some of the students' cartoon heros and favorite entertainers. Have the students explain why they admire a particular character.
2. Ask each student to which character they would most like to write a letter. It would be best to have each student write to two or three characters to be assured of receiving at least one response.
3. Since the younger students may not be able to write yet, you could type up a form letter leaving blanks after the salutation and at the bottom for the student's name and address.
4. Many of these characters will probably send 8" X 10" portraits of themselves. To help ensure a response, have the children bring in two 9" X 12" or larger envelopes; one with just a return address and the other addressed to the student. Each envelope should have at least three or four stamps on it.
5. One envelope will be used to send the letter and the S.A.S.E., while the other envelope will serve as the S.A.S.E.
6. To keep expenses at a minimum, you may want to simply mail a letter in a letter-sized envelope. In most cases, the student will still receive a reply.
7. During the school year when a student receives a reply, encourage them to bring the photo or autograph into school for show-and-tell. You may want to wait until all of the students receive a reply and have one large show-and-tell to discuss what they received.

NOTES:
1. There are many books you can use to find addresses for characters. Some of these include:

> - *The Address Book*
> - *Celebrity Register*

- Celebrity Directory: Where to Contact Over 7,000
Movie Stars, Rock Stars, Sports Stars, and Other
Famous Celebrities

2. You may want to supply the envelopes and stamps yourself. If possible, use 9" X 12" envelopes. This will allow a character to enclose a portrait of themselves.

3. Be sure to include the student's return address in the letter.

4. The S.A.S.E. can either be addressed to the student directly or have the name of the student with the school's address and be to your attention.

5. The following is a sample form letter you could use for younger students who cannot write yet:

(DATE)
Dear _____ :

    I am in (KINDERGARTEN, GRADE LEVEL). As part of a school project, I am to write to my most admired and respected character. You are my most admired character because _____
_____. I have a very special favor to ask of you. Will you please send me a personally autographed picture of yourself? It will mean a lot to me and I will share the picture with the rest of my class during show-and-tell.

    Thank you so much for taking the time to read my letter. I hope to hear from you very soon!

Sincerely,
(NAME)
(ADDRESS)

PROJECT 2

SUBJECT:
Kindergarten and Lower Grades

ASSIGNMENT:
Write to the President of the United States, First Lady, Vice President of the United States, Second Lady, or Presidential Pet.

INSTRUCTIONS:
1. Familiarize the students with the First and Second Families. You can do this by showing the students pictures and discussing the roles of each of these people.
2. Have each student choose one of the four principals of The White House to whom they would like to write a letter requesting an autograph and a biography.
3. Depending on the grade level and writing abilities, the students can either write for a signed picture or ask a question, such as "What is your favorite color?"
4. You could write a form letter for the younger students to use.
5. Because of the Franking Privilege, there is no need to send a S.A.S.E. Besides, it will be exciting for the students to receive a package in a White House envelope.

NOTES:
1. The following is the only address you will need:

> *The White House*
> *1600 Pennsylvania Avenue*
> *Washington, D.C. 20500*

2. It is possible to write to the Presidential Pet and receive a reply. Address the letter to the Pet and send it to The White House.
3. It is useless to write to the children of Presidents and Vice Presidents. A form letter is usually sent out in reply to letters for the children thanking a person for writing and explaining that because of school and other activities the children cannot personally respond to such requests.
4. Because of the thousands of similar requests The White House receives everyday, students who write to the President and Vice President will most likely receive portraits with facsimile signatures.
5. Students who write to the First Lady may be lucky and receive an authentic signature, but they, too, will probably receive a picture with a facsimile autograph.

6. Students who write to the Second Lady have the best chance of receiving a personally autographed portrait.

7. Students can request a particular picture. For example, a picture of the President and the First Lady or a picture of the Vice President's family. Pictures of Air Force I and Air Force II, which are the official planes on which the President and Vice President fly, are available. Students can also write for a portrait of The White House.

8. You may want to explain to the students that although the President and his family live at The White House, the Vice President and his family live in the Admiralty House on the grounds of the U.S. Naval Observatory about twenty minutes away from The White House. However, the Vice President and his spouse have their offices at The White House and the Old Executive Office Building(O.E.O.B.), which is right next to the President's house.

9. The following is a sample form letter you could use for the younger students:

(DATE)
Dear _____:

It is a great honor for me to be writing to you. I am a student in (KINDERGARTEN, GRADE LEVEL). We are currently learning about you and your family.

I have a very special favor to ask of you. Will you please send me a personally autographed portrait and a copy of your biography? This will mean a lot to me and I will share the picture and biography with the rest of my class.

Thank you so much for taking the time to read my letter. I hope to hear from you very soon!

Sincerely,
(NAME)
(ADDRESS)

9. Refer to "Part 1: Political Autographs"

PROJECT 3

SUBJECT:
Composition/English

ASSIGNMENT:
During a lesson in letter writing, encourage the students to write to someone whom they greatly admire. After teaching the students the format of a letter, have them write to their favorite celebrity for an autograph.

INSTRUCTIONS:
1. Have the students write as many different letters as the lesson requires. It would be best if they would send letters to at least two or three celebrities to ensure a reply.
2. Ask the students to bring in a S.A.S.E. for each request they are sending out. The size of the envelope will depend on what kind of reply the students desire: For example, a signed notecard or a signed picture.
3. If as a class you choose to all send notecards for the celebrities to sign, the envelopes can be smaller with less postage. If you choose to ask for autographed pictures, send a 9" X 12" S.A.S.E. The postage will cost more, but a picture will be more exciting to receive than a notecard.
4. Explain to the students that some celebrities receive so much mail that it is almost impossible for them to respond. For this reason, the students should choose to write to people from whom they are most likely to receive a reply.
5. Make sure the students include their home address in their letter, even if they are sending a S.A.S.E.

NOTES:
1. If possible, do this project at the beginning of the school year or a few months before summer recess so that the students will receive their autographs before school is out.
2. It would be fun to make a display in the classroom with each of the autographs as the students receive them.
3. The following is a list of sources for addresses:

- *The Who's Who Series*
- *Star Guide*
- *Celebrity Directory*
- *The Address Book*

PROJECT 4

SUBJECT:
History/Social Studies/Government

ASSIGNMENT:
  While doing a unit on the State or National Government, have each of the students write to a political official and ask for a signed photo or the students may choose to ask the politician a question.

INSTRUCTIONS:
1. Tell each of the students to whom they may write. If the class is studying the State Government, the students could write to the Governor, First Lady, Lieutenant Governor, Spouse of the Lieutenant Governor, Attorney General, Treasurer, State Senators, State Representatives, State Supreme Court Justices, or hometown mayor. If the class is studying the National Government, the students could write to the President, First Lady, Vice President, Second Lady, Cabinet Secretaries, U.S. Senators, U.S. House Members, Supreme Court Justices, former Presidents and First Ladies, former Vice Presidents and Second Ladies, and a number of other current and former politicians.
2. Teach the class about the Franking Privilege. (The Franking Privilege allows officials of the National Government and various government agencies to send out mail free of charge. The purpose of the Franking Privilege is to allow politicians to easily stay in touch with their constituents. The Franking Privilege is symbolized on the envelope by a facsimile of the official's signature in place of a stamp.)
3. Students have many options when writing to these officials. They can ask for a signed photo, biography, information on a particular issue, or a politician's position on a particular issue. The students might choose to ask an original question, such as "What is your favorite color?" or "Whom do you most admire?".
4. This project should be started early enough in the school year to allow time for a politician to reply. Each student should write to two or three politicians to ensure a response.
5. It would be fun to have a display in the classroom of the various replies the students receive.

NOTES:
1. Government offices are often very busy, so it could take several weeks for a reply.

2.   The class should be made aware of the fact that some politicians have authorized staffers who sign their signatures or that some offices use an Autopen, which mechanically copies a person's signature.   Also, be aware of facsimile signatures that appear on some portraits, especially pictures of the President.
3. The following is a list of sources for addresses:

- *The Almanac of American Politics*
- *Who's Who In America*
- *Call your Local Representative's Office*

4. Be sure to have students include their home addresses in their letters.
5. Refer to "Part 1: Political Autographs"

PROJECT 5

SUBJECT:
English/History

ASSIGNMENT:

Have each student choose a celebrity/politician they admire. The students then should research the person and write a short biography of the celebrity or a paper about why they admire the notable figure. The exact requirements of the project can be adapted for a particular subject and grade level. After the papers are completed, the students should then send them to the person about whom they are written.

INSTRUCTIONS:

1. Adapt the writing project according to the particular subject and grade level.
2. When the papers are ready to be sent, have the students write a short letter to the celebrity/politician explaining why they did the project.
3. The students have a number of options: First, the students could ask for an autographed picture; Second, the students could ask the celebrity to write back and say if they liked what was written about them; And third, the students could ask the celebrity to autograph the paper that was written about them.
4. The paper, letter, and 9" X 12" S.A.S.E. should be placed in a 9" X 12" envelope. If possible, put a piece of cardboard in the envelope to keep the paper from being bent.

NOTES:

1. Most celebrities will enjoy having students take an interest in them and they will respond to the request.
2. If the students are going to have the celebrity sign their project, be sure to put a cover sheet on each paper for the autograph. Also, the students should include a sticky tab on the page to be signed and write on the tab what they want the celebrity to sign. For example, write: "Please sign: 'To John...'"
3. The following is a list of sources for addresses:

> - *The Who's Who Series*
> - *The Address Book*
> - *The Almanac of American Politics*

PROJECT 6

<u>SUBJECT</u>:
English, History, Public Speaking

<u>ASSIGNMENT</u>:
 Have the students research a notable figure's life and causes and then write a speech to be given by that celebrity. The student can even deliver the speech as if he were the actual celebrity. The speeches should then be sent to the person for whom they were written.

<u>INSTRUCTIONS</u>:
1. The students should pick a person whom they admire and in whom they are interested.
2. The research should focus on the figure's life and the causes to which they have dedicated themselves. The goal of the research is to find a topic on which the celebrity would actually deliver a speech.
3. It would be most helpful if a student could find out the place and date of an actual speech a celebrity was delivering. For example, each year the President and First Lady deliver several commencement addresses. If the student can find out where and when one of these speeches is going to take place, then he could write the speech for that event.
4. If the speech is not for an actual event taking place, then the student should use his research to create the place, time, and purpose for the speech. For example, Tipper Gore was the Mental Health Advisor to the President's Health Care Task Force. Mrs. Gore continues to be a strong advocate for Mental Health and Homelessness issues. After discovering this through research, the student may then decide to write a speech for Mrs. Gore to be delivered at a convention for psychiatrists in New York. Another student may choose to write a speech for Michael Jordan to be delivered at a high school. The options for whom to write speeches and the subject matter are endless.
5. After the speeches are completed, the students could recite them to the entire class, while pretending to be the person for whom the speeches were written. This would give the students a great insight into what celebrities go through while preparing and delivering a speech. The class would serve as the audience for which the speech was written.
6. The student should then send a copy of their speech to the person for whom it was written, along with a letter explaining the purpose of the school project.
7. In the letters, the student can ask for the celebrity's input on the speech or

request a signed portrait. It would be fun to also ask that the copy of the speech be autographed and returned.

8. Use a 9" X 12" envelope to mail the letter and speech, along with a 9" X 12" S.A.S.E.

NOTES:

1. This project can be used for many different purposes: First, it will introduce students to the genre of speech writing; Second, through research, it will encourage students to learn more about the people they admire; Third, if the students deliver the speeches, it will give them experience in public speaking and writing for particular audiences; and Fourth, by mailing the speeches to the figures for whom they are written, the students will be given an incentive to write the speeches and they will learn about interacting with celebrities.

2. The following is a list of sources for addresses:

- *The Almanac of American Politics*
- *The Who's Who Series*

PROJECT 7

SUBJECT:
English

ASSIGNMENT:
Each student should choose one living, contemporary author to study. Have the students read a book or series of books by that author. While the students are studying a particular author of their choice, they should send that author one of his books to be autographed.

INSTRUCTIONS:
1. Have each student choose a living author to study and assign the student a certain number of books to read by that author. One book should be purchased for the student to keep. This book should be a hardcover, but can be a paperback to keep expenses at a minimum.
2. After reading one of the books, instruct the student to mail the book to the author to be signed. Together as a class, prepare the packages to be sent out.
3. There will be some expense involved with purchasing the books and postage. This cost could be divided between the school and the student.
4. The students should write a letter to the author explaining the project and asking the author to sign the book. In the letter, the student may choose to also ask the author a question, such as "What is your favorite book?"
5. Using a sticky tab, mark the page the author should autograph.
6. Get two mailing envelopes; One will be used as the S.A.S.E.
7. Address the envelopes appropriately and take them to the post office to get the Book Rate on each envelope. This will save money.
8. Be sure the envelope is securely sealed. You might want to tape or staple the envelope shut to make sure it will not open.

NOTES:
1. It will be an incentive for students to read if you tell them they can then send the books to be autographed. Perhaps, you can give extra credit for those books that are returned with autographs.
2. Be sure to use the Book Rate at the Post Office to save money on postage.
3. The following sources can be used to find addresses:

         - *The Who's Who Series*
         - *The Writer's Market*

4. If an author's direct address cannot be found, send the book in care of the publisher.

5. Refer to "Part 3: Writers' Autographs"

PROJECT 8

SUBJECT:
Religion/Theology

ASSIGNMENT:
Write to a high profile religious figure. Ask the figure a question or ask for a signed portrait and biography. This could be part of a larger project, such as a research paper or opinion paper.

INSTRUCTIONS:
1. Have each student write to a different religious figure. Examples include: The Pope, Mother Teresa, Mother Angelica, Cardinals, Bishops, Priests, Evangelists (Billy Graham and Pat Robertson), Leaders of different religions, etc...
2. Each student should write to the figure with a request for either information and/or an autograph. For example, the student could write to the Bishop of a Diocese and ask what his favorite Biblical quote is and why.
3. When the student receives a reply, he can make a presentation to the class.

NOTES:
1. If a student wants to write to the Pope, inform him that he will most likely receive a picture with a facsimile of the Pope's signature. The Pope receives thousands of similar requests and cannot personally answer each one of them. Therefore, it is not realistic to write to the Pope and ask what his favorite Biblical quote is and expect a personal reply.
2. Inform the students of the options they have regarding whom they may write.
3. The following is a list of sources for addresses:

     - Ask officials at your local church
     - The Who's Who Series

4. Refer to "Part 6: Religious Autographs"

PROJECT 9

SUBJECT:
Art

ASSIGNMENT:
Instruct each student to research a living, contemporary artist. Then, have the students create a piece of art in the style of that particular artist. When the work is completed, mail it to the artist whose style inspired the piece.

INSTRUCTION:
1. Have each student choose a living artist whose style they would like to work into a piece of their own art.
2. Each student should do extensive research on the artist and his style before beginning.
3. Each work of art must be small enough to fit into a mailing envelope.
4. After the student is finished with his work of art, he should write a letter to the artist explaining the purpose of the project.
5. In the letter, the student should request a signed picture or print. To make the project even more interesting, the student could ask the artist to inscribe something on the piece of art the student is sending.
6. When mailing the letter and work of art, be sure to pack it securely and remember to enclose a S.A.S.E.

NOTES:
1. The work of art created by the student can be from any genre of art, including drawing, painting, sculpture, cartoons, clothing design, architecture, interior design, and photography.
2. The following is a list of sources to find addresses:

- *Who's Who in America*
- *Who's Who in American Art*

3. Refer to "Part 4: Artists' Autographs"

PROJECT 10

SUBJECT:
Art

ASSIGNMENT:
      Instruct each student to choose their favorite living artist. The student should send the artist a blank piece of canvas board or drawing paper and ask the artist to doodle or draw something for them.

INSTRUCTION:
1. Each student should research several living artists and choose one or two of their favorites.
2. Write a letter to the artist explaining that this is a school project and ask them to draw or doodle on a piece of canvas board or drawing paper. It is important to specify that this is for a school project. The artist may be more willing to comply with your request if he knows it is for educational purposes.
3. Mail the letter, canvas board or paper, and a S.A.S.E. to the artist. Be sure to securely pack the materials so they will not be damaged.
4. A slight variation to this project could be to write celebrities who are not exclusively artists and ask them to doodle or draw something for you.
5. To figure out how much postage will be, take the package to the post office to be weighed and stamped.

NOTES:
1. It is best to use canvas board because it is sturdy and comes in a variety of sizes.
2. Be creative with the project. For example, you could ask an artist to draw a flower.
3. The following is a list of sources for addresses:

        - *Who's Who in America*
        - *Who's Who in America Art*

4. Refer to "Part 4: Artists' Autographs"

PROJECT 11

SUBJECT:
Art

ASSIGNMENT:
Design a new logo or trademark for an existing company or product. Mail the design to the President of the company or to the designer of the existing logo.

INSTRUCTIONS:
1. Choose an existing company or product for which to design a logo or symbol. For example, design a new logo for the fashion designer Calvin Klein or for the restaurant Wendy's.
2. Once the logo is completed, mail it to the company or designer for whom you created it and ask for their input. For example, mail the logo to Calvin Klein or send the Wendy's logo to its founder, Dave Thomas.
3. Write a letter explaining the school project along with your request. Also, remember to enclose a S.A.S.E. and securely pack the design so it is not damaged.
4. Ask the person to whom you are sending the logo for their autograph or ask them to inscribe comments on your design and send it back.
5. Take the package to the post office to be weighed and to have postage put on the S.A.S.E.

NOTES:
1. Be creative with the logos and to whom they are sent.
2. The following is a list of sources for addresses:

- *The Who's Who Series*
- *The Address Book*
- *Celebrity Directory*

PROJECT 12

SUBJECT:
Art

ASSIGNMENT:
Have each student choose one of their favorite celebrities. Then, instruct the students to draw either a caricature or portrait of that celebrity. Once the caricatures are completed, send the drawings to the celebrities to be autographed and sent back to the students.

INSTRUCTIONS:
1. Each student should choose a favorite celebrity to draw. Inform the students that they have a better chance of getting responses from certain celebrities than from others.
2. The drawings should be done on a sturdy board that will not be damaged in the mail.
3. Write a letter to the celebrity explaining the purpose of the school project and ask them to personally autograph the sketch and send it back. Be sure to enclose a S.A.S.E. in with the drawing.
4. To ensure proper postage, take the packages to the post office to be weighed and stamped.

NOTES:
1. The following is a list of sources for addresses:

   - *Who's Who in America*
   - *The Address Book*

PROJECT 13

SUBJECT:
Science

ASSIGNMENT:
Each student should choose one outstanding, living member of the science community and study the person's life and achievements as a research project. As part of the research, the students should write to the notable, scientific figure they are studying. At the end, the research along with the personal response can be compiled into a paper or other project and presented to the class.

INSTRUCTIONS:
1. Have each student choose a living person who has made a contribution to science. For example, the student may choose a Nobel Prize winner, a famous doctor, an inventor, a chemist, an environmentalist, or some other famous scientist.
2. The student should then research their subject's life and work. Since most of these scientists will be from the last few decades, the students should use news clips as well as other books and encyclopedias for their research.
3. As part of the research, the student should write a letter to their scientist and tell them about the school project on which they are working. The student should then ask the scientist for a statement about his or her life's work to be used in the school project. Be sure to also ask for an autographed picture, if one is available.
4. Include a S.A.S.E. It would be best to send 9" X 12" envelopes.
5. Send the letters several weeks or months before the actual project is due. This will allow the scientist enough time to respond.

NOTES:
1. There are many possibilities to whom the students may write. The students should not be limited to only famous and well-known scientists. The project can be just as educational and as beneficial to the students if they write to lesser known inventors, chemists, etc... Many companies have these types of people working for them and they would probably be more than willing to cooperate with a school project.
2. The following is a list of sources for addresses:

> - *Who's Who in Science & Engineering*
> - *Who's Who in Science in Europe*

PROJECT 14

SUBJECT:
High School Level

ASSIGNMENT:
Since many high schools require service/volunteer hours as part of their course curriculum, students should be encouraged to work at places where they will be in contact with high profile figures. This will be an extra incentive for the students to volunteer their services.

INSTRUCTIONS:
1. Supply the students with a list of exciting places in your area at which they could complete their service hours.
2. Discuss why working at such places could be educational and fun. For example, the place the student chooses might be frequented by celebrities who offer their services for charity.
3. When the service hours are completed, the student can give a presentation to the class, discussing the people he met and what he learned.

NOTES:
1. Unfortunately, not all areas have places where famous people work and visit. Local and state government offices and local charity organizations are exciting places for students to volunteer their services. For example, it could be just as beneficial to a student to volunteer his services in a hometown mayor's office.
2. If a student volunteers at the right place, he will be able to get autographs and other signed items and memorabilia.

PROJECT 15

SUBJECT:
College Internships

ASSIGNMENT:
      Many colleges require students to complete internships as part of their majors. Internships can be either boring and tedious or thrilling and educational. A student should choose an internship that suits his interests and offers a wide range of experiences.

INSTRUCTIONS:
1. Inform students of the possibilities available for internships. Specifically, tell students about internships at which they will be in contact with notable figures. For example, the most exciting internships are available at The White House and on Capitol Hill. In New York or Los Angeles, interning at a studio or celebrity agency would be a most thrilling experience for a college student.
2. Have the students choose where they would like to intern and then contact the place for an application or list of requirements.

NOTES:
1. By interning at such places, a student will learn more about people and business than any textbook can teach them.
2. Internships usually offer great work experience for students and look very impressive on resumes.

AUTHOR'S NOTE:
      During my Senior year at Marymount University in Arlington, Virginia, I interned with Mrs. Tipper Gore's Communications Director/Press Secretary, Sally Aman, in the Office of the Vice President at The White House. This experience was invaluable to me. I learned more in those eight months than any college course could have taught me. I was fortunate to be placed with Sally, because she truly is the best at what she does. It is important to figure out what you like to do and then work with someone who does it well. That is how you learn the most!

Part 10

A.S.A.P.

Americans for a Sound AIDS/HIV Policy

P.O. Box 17433 ◆ Washington, D.C. 20041 ◆ Telephone: 703/471-7350 ◆ Fax: 703/471-8409

December 4, 1995

Mr. Patrick Jephson
Private Secretary to H.R.H.
The Princess of Wales
St. James's Palace
London SW1A 1BS
England

Dear Madam,

    I was thrilled recently when I saw a speech Your Royal
Highness delivered discussing Ma'am's utmost concern for the
children whose parents are infected and dying of AIDS.

    My wife, Anita, and I share this concern with Ma'am. In
1988, we founded the ASAP Children's Assistance Fund. We provide
counseling, emergency financial assistance, a care-givers
network, and a holiday gift program.

    Our holiday gift program is our most visible activity as we
raise money to buy holiday gifts for children who are both
infected and affected by the AIDS epidemic. Virtually all of
these children will eventually be orphaned. We started by
serving 2 children and now we deliver gifts to more than 10,000
children all over the United States.

    As an international ambassador and patron of this cause, I
feel that the Children's Assistance Fund is a group in which
Ma'am would be most interested.

    We would be honored to join forces with Ma'am to help the
most often forgotten victims of this epidemic--the children.

    The ASAP Children's Assistance Fund is hosting a "Nurture
the Little Ones" benefit dinner in Washington, D.C. on December
13, 1995. It would be a distinct pleasure if Ma'am could join us
should Ma'am be in Washington at that time.

    If Ma'am is unable to attend, we would very much like to
work with Ma'am on future projects. If Ma'am would like more
information about the ASAP Children's Assistance Fund, please
feel free to contact our office at 703-471-7350.

    I have the honor to be, Madam, your Royal Highness's most
humble and obedient servant.

                         W. Shepherd Smith, Jr.
                         President

Dedicated to limiting total suffering from AIDS/HIV.

**This is the proper way to write a letter to royalty.
Luckily, writing for autographs is a bit easier.**

CHAPTER 18
WRITING A LETTER

There are several tips for writing letters to celebrities. The most important rule to follow when writing for an autograph is to keep your letter short and to the point. The following is a list of other guidelines to consider when writing to famous people for their signatures:

♦ Keep letters short: 1 - 2 pages. Even though you are writing the letter to a particular celebrity, usually the celebrity's staff will first read the letter and decide what to do with it.

♦ It is best to neatly handwrite the letters.

♦ If your handwriting is bad, type the letters.

♦ Appropriately address the person to whom you are writing by using Mr., Mrs., Ms., or another professional title. Since most famous women keep their same last name after marriage, address them as Ms.

♦ Address elected officials according to their position: For example, Senator..., Congresswoman..., Secretary..., or Prime Minister...

♦ Begin the letter by complimenting the person to whom you are writing: For example, "It is a honor to be writing to you. You are my most admired actor of all time!"

♦ State the purpose of your letter in a concise manner: For example, "I am working on a school project studying the U.S. Supreme Court. Will you please send me a personally signed portrait of yourself for my project?"

♦ Be sure to frequently use "Please" and "Thank You".

♦ End your letter by thanking the celebrity for reading your letter and let them know you are anxiously awaiting a reply.

♦ Print your name and address at the bottom or top of the letter.

♦ Always date your letter.

♦ You can be creative using bright stationery and colored pens.

♦ To ensure a response, enclose a S.A.S.E.

♦ If you are sending an item to be signed, specify what you want signed and where you would like the celebrity to sign it: For example, enclose a sticky tab saying, "Please sign: 'To John'".

♦ Always put your return address on the envelope.

♦ Be sure to put enough postage on the envelope. If you are unsure of the postage, take the envelope to the post office to be weighed and stamped. This is especially helpful when mailing books because of the Book Rate.

♦ To mail out a large amount of form letters, use mail merge on a computer.

The following is a sample letter you can use when writing for autographs:

(DATE)
Dear Mrs. Bush:

It is a great honor for me to be writing to you. You are one of my most admired First Ladies of all time!

I have a very special favor to ask of you. Will you please send me a personally autographed portrait of yourself? It will mean the world to me and I will always treasure it!

Thank you so much for reading my letter. I have enclosed a S.A.S.E. for you to use. I hope to hear from you very soon!

Sincerely,

John E. Schlimm II
479 Brussells St.
St. Marys, PA 15857

CHAPTER 19
FINDING ADDRESSES

There are many sources for finding addresses of the rich and famous. The most reliable sources I use are <u>Who's Who in America</u> and <u>The Address Book</u>. The <u>Who's Who</u> series of books includes an endless variety of volumes highlighting the most notable figures in the various categories, including politicians, writers, artists, media stars, businessmen, musicians, foreign leaders, religious figures, and other outstanding personalities.

It is very important to use the most updated address book available. For example, <u>Who's Who in America</u> is published every year and <u>The Almanac of American Politics</u> is published every two years. Celebrity addresses are constantly changing and, therefore, you must find current address books. If you cannot find a celebrity's direct address, you can also write to them in care of agents, studios, publishers, political offices, and any other organizations with which the figure is associated.

You should check at your local library or bookstore for books with celebrity addresses. The following is a list of address sources to get you started on your collection:

<u>ADDRESS SOURCES</u>:

1. <u>Who's Who in America</u>
2. <u>Who's Who among Black Americans</u>
3. <u>Who's Who in American Art</u>
4. <u>Who's Who in American Politics</u>
5. <u>Who's Who in Religion</u>
6. <u>Who's Who in Rock & Roll</u>
7. <u>Who's Who in Science & Engineering</u>
8. <u>Who's Who in Television</u>
9. <u>Who's Who of American Inventors</u>
10. <u>Who's Who of American Women</u>
11. <u>Who's Who of Nobel Prize Winners</u>
12. <u>Who's Who in American Theatre</u>
13. <u>The Almanac of American Politics</u>
14. <u>Celebrity Directory</u>
15. <u>Star Guide</u>
16. <u>Social Register</u>
17. <u>The Address Book</u>

18. <u>Writer's Market</u>
19. Local Representative's Office
20. State Capitol
21. U.S. Capitol
22. The White House

CHAPTER 20
ADDRESSES TO GET YOU STARTED

The White House
1600 Pennsylvania Avenue, N.W.
Washington, D.C. 20500

The Supreme Court of the United States
1 First Street, N.E.
Washington, D.C. 20501

The U.S. Senate
Washington, D.C. 20510

The U.S. House of Representatives
Washington, D.C. 20515

President and Mrs. Jimmy Carter
The Carter Center
One Copenhill
Atlanta, Georgia 30307

President and Mrs. Reagan
11000 Wilshire Boulevard
Los Angeles, California 90024

President and Mrs. Bush
10000 Memorial Drive
Houston, Texas 77024

The Pope
Apostolic Palace
00120 Vatican City
                    Italy

The British Royal Family
Buckingham Palace
London, England

British Prime Minister
10 Downing Street
London SW1A 2AA
                England

CNN
One CNN Center
Atlanta, Georgia 30348

NBC
30 Rockefeller Plaza
New York, New York 10112

ABC
77 West 66th Street
New York, New York 10023

CBS
524 West 57th Street
New York, New York 10019

Mr. Fred Rogers
Mister Rogers' Neighborhood
Family Communications, Inc.
4802 Fifth Avenue
Pittsburgh, Pennsylvania 15213

Miss America
Miss America Organization
P.O. Box 119
Atlantic City, New Jersey 08404

Mother Teresa
Missionaries of Charity
54/A, A. J. C. Bose Road
Calcutta - 700016. India

CHAPTER 21
STORING AND DISPLAYING AUTOGRAPHS

Once you have gone through the work of obtaining an autograph, either in person or through the mail, you want to ensure that it will be protected. I store most of my autographs in plastic sheet protectors and binders. Each binder represents a different genre. If autographs are in sheet protectors, you do not have to worry about people directly touching them. Be sure to use acid free sheet protectors to help preserve the autographs even longer.

Although it may not be possible to frame all of your autographs, I have a few of my favorite signatures hanging on the wall, especially the signed pictures of me with a celebrity. It is nice to matte and frame a signed picture or letter. Be sure to use acid free matte to protect the autograph. When placing an autographed picture or letter in a matte, use tape not glue. This way, if you ever want to remove the autograph from the matte, it will be easy to do. The most important point to remember when framing autographs is to not hang the autograph in direct sunlight, which will fade the signature over time. Framed autographs make a wonderful decorating theme for bedrooms, family rooms, offices, and just about any other place you might want to hang them.

If you have objects signed, such as T-shirts, baseballs, basketballs, hats, and books, you can show them in display cases. Books can be framed and hung on the wall. There are actual display cases especially designed for baseballs and basketballs available at hobby stores. Once again, be sure to avoid placing the signed objects in direct sunlight.

It is a good idea to keep a record of the celebrities to whom you write, the responses you receive, and your expenses for postage, envelopes, etc...

CHAPTER 22
A CHECKLIST FOR COLLECTING AUTOGRAPHS

The following is a checklist of points to remember when collecting autographs:

- Focus on collecting your favorite genre of autographs.
- Use the most up-to-date address books.
- Handwrite the letters if possible.
- Always put your address in the letter and on the envelope.
- Keep letters short and to the point.
- Start the letter by complimenting the celebrity.
- Besides an autograph, ask for a biography of the celebrity.
- Send items for a celebrity to sign (Ex/ Book). A lot of celebrities who will not send out autographs in response to general requests will sign copies of their books.
- Find celebrities' books on bargain piles at bookstores or at Resale shops. Also, watch at your local bookstore for celebrity book signings.
- When mailing books, take the book to the post office to be weighed and stamped using the Book Rate, which is cheaper than regular postage rates.
- When mailing books or other items to be signed, it is always a good idea to enclose a Self-Addressed, Stamped Envelope (S.A.S.E.).
- It is unnecessary to send a S.A.S.E. to most U.S. politicians because they have the Franking Privilege.
- Keep a record of everyone to whom you write.
- Ask a celebrity to write a particular inscription.
- Ask the celebrity a question.
- Address the celebrity appropriately (Ex/ Your Majesty).
- When writing foreign leaders, always write U.S.A. under your address.
- Write to the same celebrity several times to see what responses you will receive.
- Autographs are very educational and can be incorporated into numerous school projects.
- If you do a school project about a celebrity, mail the project to the person about whom it is written.
- Save everything a celebrity sends to you, including the envelope.
- Some celebrities will try to get you to join their fan club. Beware of these

responses because they usually ask for a membership fee.

- ♦   If you have the opportunity to meet a celebrity, ask for his or her autograph. It is best to use a Sharpie Fine Point Permanent Marker. Also, get your picture taken with the celebrity and mail it to them to sign.
- ♦   The only way to be sure your autograph is authentic is to get it in person. Celebrities have staffs who are authorized to sign a celebrity's signature and some notable figures use Autopens or facsimile signatures on pictures.
- ♦   If at first you do not get an authentic autograph or response of any kind, keep writing until you do get one.
- ♦   Preserve your autographs in sheet protectors and binders or by framing and hanging them. Do not let people touch them and keep the signatures out of direct sunlight.

Above all, have fun with your hobby. You will find it to be both rewarding and educational!

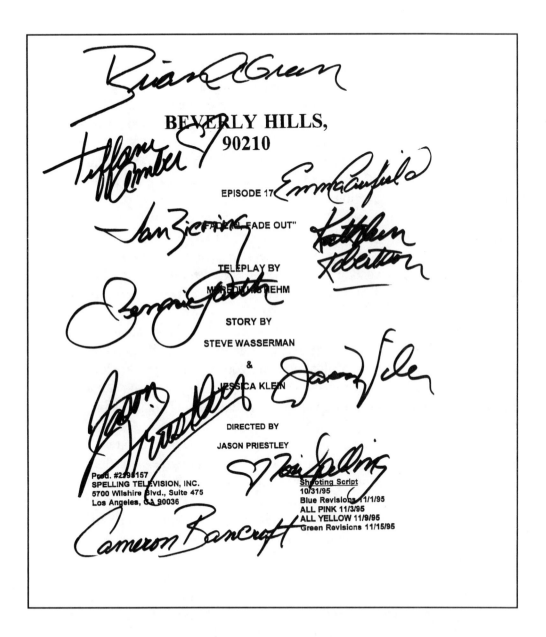

Part 11

One of my autograph auction purchases

CHAPTER 23
AUTOGRAPHS FOR AUCTION

In the past year, I have engaged in a new facet of autographs: Autograph and Celebrity Memorabilia Auctions. These events are very fun to help organize and run.

During September 1995, I started volunteering at the ASAP Children's Assistance Fund headquartered in Herndon, Virginia. The charity in part raises money to buy holiday gifts for children who are infected and affected by the AIDS epidemic. Each of these children will eventually be orphaned. I helped with special events and press relations.

My main job was to help plan a December 13th "Nurture The Little Ones" fundraising dinner in Washington, D.C. As part of the dinner, I organized a silent, celebrity memorabilia auction.

Autograph and memorabilia auctions are a great way for a nonprofit organization to raise money. The auctions can either be silent, meaning bids are placed on a bid sheet by prospective buyers, or an auctioneer can be brought in for a more lively, open auction. Most celebrities are very generous when it comes to donating personal memorabilia for good causes. And, these items can fetch very high donations on the auction block!

There are a few things you have to consider when planning an auction. You must decide on an appropriate location and the type of auction that will take place. If you are planning a silent auction, you have to choose a location with enough table space for the items to be properly displayed. If the auction will be conducted by an auctioneer, there must be enough seating and standing room for the participants.

Next, you must decide to which celebrities you will send letters. I suggest sending letters to as broad a range of celebrities as possible. For the Children's Fund auction, I sent out more than 500 letters to well known figures in a variety of fields, including Hollywood stars, singing stars, Presidential personalities, business figures, religious figures, media people, athletes, and various other government officials. However, your auction could have a theme, such as all authors or all sports figures. That would also be very fun!

Once you decide to whom you will write, you must then decide how you are going to package your organization or cause. Along with my cover letter requesting a personally signed piece of personal memorabilia, a toy for the children, or a statement to be read at the dinner, I also included a drawing from an infected child and an old newsletter. Other items that might be included in such packets are fact sheets or other background information on the organization.

In the cover letter, be sure to clearly state a deadline date by which all of the items should be sent to you! Since celebrities have very busy schedules, allow as much time as possible for them to respond to your request. The response time should be at least one to three months.

The most fun you will have with any memorabilia auction is waiting for the items to come in the mail and then opening them. At ASAP, we all gathered in my office while I opened the packages and envelopes. For a month, it was like Christmas everyday!

One of the most important things to keep in mind when doing an auction is to stay as organized as possible. As the items for the Children's Fund auction started to come in, I recorded what we received and who had sent it. This was immediately followed-up with a thank you note.

If a letter is sent back because of a wrong address, record the correction on your master list so you do not send a letter to that address the next time. If a response comes back from an address which is different from the address to which you originally sent the request, record the new address. It is probably a more direct way of reaching the particular celebrity.

I was so surprised by the variety of responses we received. A few of the autographed items we got included books from Pat Buchanan, Senator Jesse Helms, Joe Paterno, Mary Fisher, Sue Grafton, Mary Kay Ash, Dudley Moore, Dave Thomas, Sherri Lewis, Siegfried & Roy, Martha Stewart, and Dr. Ralph Reed, Jr.; portraits from Astronaut Frank Borman, Dan Quayle, Charlton Heston, Bob Hope, Richard Petty, and Naomi Judd; photographs from artists Christo & Jeanne-Claude; Presidential Memorabilia from Jimmy Carter, George and Barbara Bush, and Ronald and Nancy Reagan; and sports memorabilia from The Washington Redskins, Muhammad Ali, Monica Seles, Terry Bradshaw, Dan Jansen, and Bonnie Blair.

I found that many celebrities who will not respond to a general request for an autograph will respond for a charitable cause. Also, if you have contacts who know celebrities or if you know any well known figures yourself, utilize that contact and get items for your auction. At the Children's Fund, we were fortunate to have several people who knew celebrities or had special contacts. One contact was able to get us several items signed by The Washington Redskins.

Some celebrities and organizations will respond by saying that they cannot send anything either because of the extraordinary number of requests they receive or because they only support certain charities in their state. Many sports teams responded to my requests in this manner, which was disappointing, yet understandable.

If portraits are sent, they should be put in plastic sheet protectors. The other items should be left in the mailing envelopes to protect them. Beware of

Autopen signatures and forgeries on photos and the other items. Believe it or not, some celebrities will send items that they say are autographed, but they are not authentic. These items should be marked as such when auctioned.

After all of the items are received, it is then a good idea for you to have them appraised by an autograph dealer. This should be done for tax purposes for your organization, the celebrity, and the person buying the item. And, it will give you an idea of what the starting bid should be. It is also a good idea to consult an accountant about how your organization should go about handling the auction financially.

You should write a list of the items to be handed out before the auction so people can get an idea on what they would like to bid. The bidding sheets which will accompany a silent auction item need to include all of the information about the item since they will be placed on the table with the item. Bidding sheets should include the following: Description of the item, starting bid, the raise, space for the bidder's name or bidder's number, closing time, and method and time of payment and pick-up. Some people would advise listing the appraised value. I advise using it as a guideline for starting bids, but do not list it. Perhaps then, people will bid higher than if they would have known what the real price was.

The raise is the amount of money that has to be added to an old bid in order to make the new bid. For example, an item with a starting bid of $100.00 could have a raise of $20.00. Therefore, if someone bids $100.00, then the next person has to bid $120.00.

Also, instead of asking bidders to list their names, you might encourage more bidding if every person is given a code number to use. This way, the bidders can remain anonymous and may feel more comfortable to place bids. This is especially true if you are having famous people attend your event. They can bid without everyone knowing about it.

Silent auctions need a lot of supervision. It is wise to station one worker or volunteer for every ten to fifteen items. The worker can then answer any questions about the items and watch over them.

It is also very important to close the auction when you said you would. This will avoid a lot of confusion and hurt feelings later. It could be fun to take the top few items and have a live auction during your event.

Once the auction is closed, organize the bidding sheets into alphabetical order according to the last name or code number of the winning bidder. This way, when the people start asking if they got a certain item it will be easy to find out. The sheets can then be divided into several pick-up stations.

Be sure to give each buyer a receipt for tax purposes. I did learn, however, that auction donations at political fundraisers are not tax deductible. Regardless of the type of auction, it is good public relations to follow-up an auction with thank you notes to all of the buyers. This may encourage them to donate in the future.

And, just to demonstrate how fun and adventurous autograph and memorabilia auctions can be, I have a story about the Children's Assistance Fund auction on which I worked. On the Friday before the auction, I got a phone call. The voice on the other end said: "Hello, this is Alma Powell!" For those of you who do not recognize that name from earlier in this book, Alma Powell is the wife of General Colin Powell. She said that she had a copy of her husband's book, signed by both of them, for our auction and could someone please pick it up.

Mrs. Powell gave me her home address and I told her I would pick the book up before noon. I grabbed my friend Stephanie, who works at the Children's Assistance Fund, and we were off. We rang the door bell when we arrived and a few seconds later Mrs. Powell opened the door. She invited us into her living room. All of a sudden, I found myself sitting in Colin Powell's living room when just a few months earlier I had stood for three hours in line to have him sign a copy of his book! It never ceases to amaze me where one might end up from one minute to the next in Washington, D.C.!

I hope when you have your autograph auction, you find it to be as fun, exciting, adventurous, and rewarding as mine was! Good luck!

GLOSSARY

AUTOGRAPH - A person's signature written in his
handwriting.

AUTOPEN - A machine that mechanically copies a person's
signature.

BOOK RATE - A special rate of postage the post office gives
when mailing books.

BOOK PLATE - An autographed sticker placed in a book.

FRANKING PRIVILEGE - Allows members of Congress and
other officials and agencies of
the national government to send
out mail free of charge. This is
signified by the official's
signature in place of a stamp.

GENRE - A particular category of autographs. For Example, larger
genres include Political, Media, Sports, and Famous Families;
smaller genres include Presidents, First Ladies, Newscasters,
Country Singers, and Lawyers.

GRAPHOLOGY - The study of handwriting.

FACSIMILE -A copy of a signature.

MAIL MERGE - A computer option for mass-producing form letters; it can be
very helpful when writing the same letter to several
celebrities for autographs (Ex/ All 100 U.S. Senators).

S.A.S.E. - Self-Addressed, Stamped Envelope.

EPILOGUE

In the end, no matter what people think or say,
I want to know in my heart that I did it my way!

If you have my book and would like me to autograph it for you, I would be more than happy to reply. Then you will have the authentic autograph of a serious autograph collector!

I do ask that you send a S.A.S.E. though as I have used all my envelopes and stamps to write for more autographs!

Here's to the future...

John E. Schlimm II
479 Brussells Street
St. Marys, Pennsylvania 15857

December 1, 1995

ACKNOWLEDGEMENTS

I would like to thank the following people for their contributions to this book:

Roland R. Foster, who shared a lot of this history with me even though we were often on different sides!

Dr. Janet Fallon, who originally encouraged me to send the Barbara Bush speech to The White House from which I received my first autograph.

Mrs. Mary Meyer, who is truly a First Lady of Grammar! Everything I know about writing started with her.

Mr. Jake Meyer, who shared his expertise as a lawyer with me.

Mom and Dad, who have supported and encouraged me throughout this entire process.

Sally Aman and Mrs. Tipper Gore, who both gave me one of the best years of my life! They are both a great inspiration behind this book.

W. Shepherd and Anita Smith, who are two of the kindest and most generous people I know!

My Friends, who keep me young at heart!

And finally, thank you most of all to every celebrity who has sent me their "authentic" autograph. You are the greatest inspiration behind this book!